Stagecoach Lines & Freighters of

West Texas

By

Barbara Barton

ISBN 978-0-6151-9920-7

The picture on the cover is courtesy of West Texas Collection, Angelo State University.

Barton's Books

P.O. Box 6

Knickerbocker, Texas 76939

Phone: (325) 949-7303

e-mail: bba7303@aol.com

website: http://www.bartonbooks.net

Dedication

I dedicate this book to the many stagecoach builders, drivers, and helpers who made this method of transportation possible. I also have a soft spot in my heart for freighters because my granddaddy Dave Gentry was one of those men who brought supplies to the ranchers with his wagon. I dedicate this book to them also.

Table of Contents

Preface

My interest in stagecoach lines began when my Dad explained the deep ruts imbedded in limestone rocks in our pasture. He said they were made by a stage that traveled between Sherwood and Ozona, Texas. At the time, I was a teenager chasing sheep in that pasture. It was more fun to look at the stage road than corral those sheep. Years later, I decided to collect stories about the stages that drove over our pasture, as well as other parts of West Texas, and put them in this book.

Many people have helped me in this search for historical facts. Dewayne Vinson assisted my visit to Camp Charlotte where the stage passed along the Butterfield Trail. Jim Ridge took me over the rocky hills of the M. D. Bryant Ranch so I could see the stage sign that still reads "S. A. 23 mi." Suzanne Campbell with the West Texas Collection, Angelo State University, helped me find materials as well as pictures. Mrs. Margaret Waring of the Comanche County Library directed me to stagecoach stories of that area.

Members of the Crockett County Museum provided a picture for me. Bob Tate gave me pictures of the Pinery Stage Stop in the Guadalupe Mountains. "Thank you's" also go to Sharon Gentry and Larry Anderson for reading my manuscript.

Interesting stories about the stage drivers came from Troy Williams and the family of W. A. Pringle. But my number one helper was my husband, Lewis, who listened to my stories over and over. He patiently stopped often to take roadside pictures. Thanks to all of you.

I am available to give talks about stagecoach lines to clubs and groups.

Stagecoach road through my Dad's pasture looking southward. Picture was taken in the 1980's. This road initiated my interest in stagecoach lines. Photo is in author's collection.

Chapter 1: San Antonio to El Paso

In the early 1850s, there were few stagecoaches bouncing along the windswept trails of West Texas. The only noticeable movement on most prairies came from cattle herds heading north or bands of marauding Indians, kicking up as much trouble as possible.

Unless a person owned horses or a good wagon and team, the Lower Route of the San Antonio to El Paso Stage Line was the sole transportation that travelers could hop on to cross the southern edge of West Texas. This route left San Antonio and passed through Fort Stockton, Coyanosa, Limpia River to Fort Davis, Barrell Springs, Van Horn, Eagle Spring, Ft. Quitman, Fort Hancock, San Elizario Army Post and into Franklin, later called El Paso.

On September 20, 1851, Henry Skillman was granted a contract to provide mail service from San Antonio to Santa Fe by way of El Paso. His first mailbags departed on November 3, 1851. A few weeks later, Skillman had a stage moving along the same trail. By 1857, he offered passenger service from San Antonio to San Diego, a trip that usually took twenty-seven or more days. A passenger making this trip and eating at the stage stops would expect to cough up $200 for a one-way trip.

Henry Skillman had good men helping him as he traversed the countryside full of Indians and outlaws. William "Big Foot" Wallace was one of his drivers when Skillman's stage made its first run to Limpia Canyon, near Fort Davis. This tall, muscular man named Wallace was as much a legend in Texas as Paul Bunyan was in the northern territories. E. P. Webster from Illinois and Diedrick Dutchover, a Belgian immigrant, escorted Wallace on his maiden voyage through the Davis Mountains. Weeks later, Webster became the manager of the Limpia Canyon stage stand while Dutchover worked as a stage guard. Dutchover kept this route for two years.

Big Foot Wallace fought with Texans in 1842 and wore the title of Texas Ranger many years before he started driving stagecoaches. The Texas Rangers who he commanded battled border bandits and Indians over a wide region of Texas, so he knew what he was signing up for when he drove the stage toward the Davis Mountains. Wallace walked many miles to El Paso one time after Indians stole his mules.

The story of his long trek reveals that he finally found some food at a home

---

San Antonio to Fort Stockton Stage Line

Toyahville   Fort Stockton

Ft. Davis

Camp Hudson

Comstock

Del Rio   San Antonio

Eagle Pass

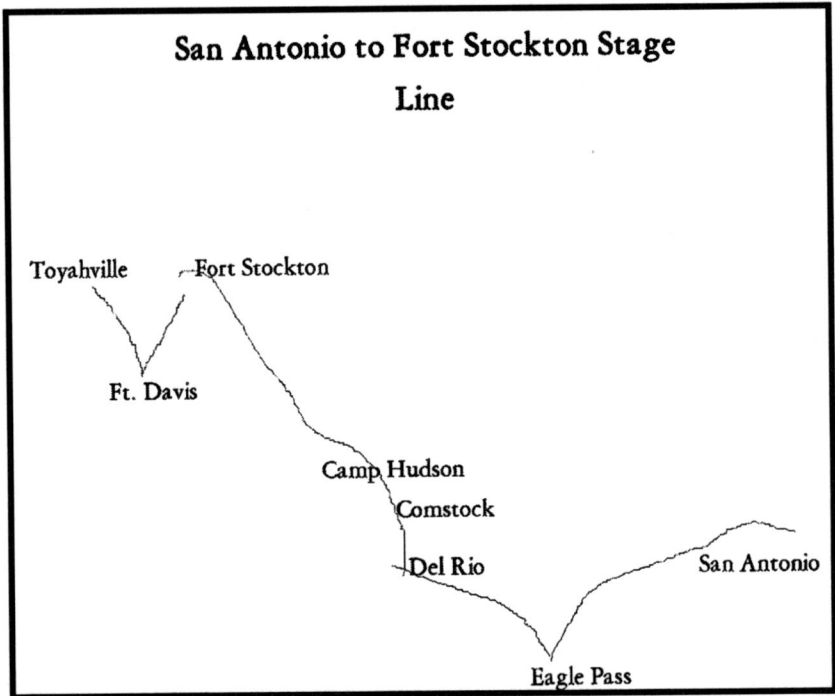

near El Paso. He ate 27 eggs at that table and finished the day with a complete meal at a later time when he hit El Paso. Wallace was six foot two inches tall and 240 pounds of all muscle.

While Skillman owned this contract, he established four stage stands in Jeff Davis County. Fort Davis opened in 1854 to protect these travelers in the Davis Mountains, but by April of that year, Skillman lost the stage contract. It was given to David Wasson, but he wasn't dependable. When he failed to deliver the stages in a timely manner, his boss looked for another contractor. The next stage owner was George Giddings who decided to try his hand at running a stage between San Antonio and El Paso.

Up to this time, Giddings was known as the man behind the counter at his store. George Giddings, clerk of the C. J. Cook & Company store in San Antonio in 1847, liked his worked so much that he bought the San Antonio store as well as the one in El Paso two years later. For the next twelve years, Giddings owned both stores and decided to also operate the San Antonio-Santa Fe Line in 1854. George Giddings soon discovered that the route between San Antonio and El Paso was the most

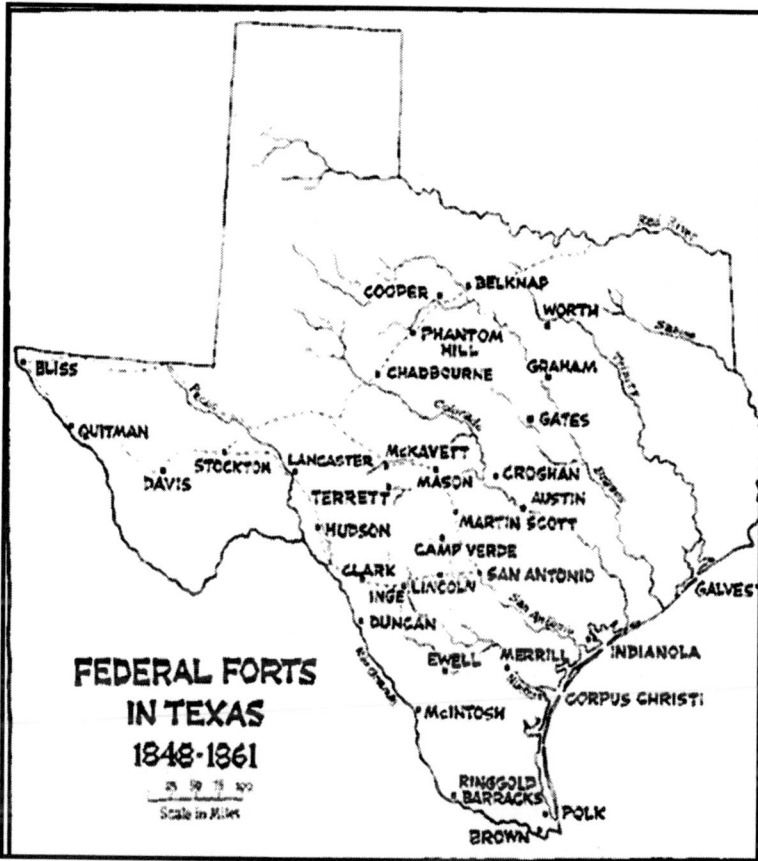

FEDERAL FORTS
IN TEXAS
1848-1861

Scale in Miles

dangerous of all. He managed his 1,100-miles route with one six-mule team, thirty-six more mules scattered between the stations, and a guard of seven men.

Although this venture was supposed to make money, Giddings soon found otherwise. In the year 1855, he lost 270 mules and sixty horses due to Indian raids. Through the years he lost supplies, livestock, and some stage stations. All of these had to be replaced to keep the line going.

Giddings secured help in running the stages with the "Jackass Mail" by partnering with James Birch on June 22, 1857. Birch bought the San Antonio-San Diego Mail Contract while George and M. B. Bramhall acted as his agents. Giddings took care of the route from San Antonio to El Paso. Birch died within a year and Giddings bought his share from Birch's widow.

As sole owner of the stage line. Giddings continued to lose money, and the competition between his line and that of Butterfield's finally destroyed his business. Loss from Indian raids was his main problem, so he asked for reimbursement by pleading his case in Washington. In the late 1800s, many ranchers were compensated by the government for their huge losses in cattle due to Indian theft. Similiar depredation cases were filed by ranchers who later received government funds, but no such money was available for stage owners. The government disallowed Gidding's claims because he had not personally witnessed his many losses.

The travelers on this lower route dealt with Indians and outlaws, so the government established Fort Lancaster August 21, 1856. Soldiers assigned to this post found themselves in a desolate area ten miles east of what is now known as Sheffield. The area was desert-like with a little sagebrush and cacti to break the monotony of seeing little else. Foothills of limestone towered in the distance as troops rode scouting trails.

Capt. Stephen D. Carpenter brought companies H and K to Camp Lancaster when most everybody slept in picket-canvas houses. Eventually the fort's officer quarters and barracks were built with limestone rocks or adobe. The government had a temporary building called "Turnley prefabricated building," which was used also for a period of time at this fort. The location where Capt. Stephen D. Carpenter of the U. S. Infantry setup Camp Lancaster was one mile northeast of the point where Live Oak Creek flowed into the Pecos River. An old government road passed through this camp later known as Fort Lancaster.

On May 27, 1857, Second Lt. John Sherburne of the 1st[st] Infantry wrote a letter to Major Vinton, Chief of Quartermaster. In his letter, he mentioned that Fort Lancaster now included a commissary, storehouse, hospital, five officer quarters, commanding Officer's Quarters, two barracks, a baker house, a blacksmith shop, a guardhouse, a forage house, a harness house, and two company kitchens. As the fort developed over time, it included 25 buildings and a large rectangular parade ground.

Soldiers stationed at Fort Lancaster had the job of protecting the stage from Indian attacks. Some stages had guards in addition to the soldiers. One Mexican guard told the tale of his stage waiting at the bottom of Lancaster Hill until Cavalry guards met

Map showing the San Antonio-San Diego Stage Route from San Antonio to Fort Stockton.

them. As they waited, they saw another stage coming down the hill with rifle shots firing all around it. Indians were chasing them. The soldiers usually met that stage also, but on that particular day, they missed them. The road was smoother than expected down the hill because the soldiers hauled dirt every day of the year, trying to keep it in good shape.

Most of the soldiers rode mules at this fort as they also protected wagon trains on the San Antonio-El Paso "lower road." Capt. Robert Granger was in command of Fort Lancaster on March 19, 1861, when the post was abandoned to the Confederates. This post never officially opened again. However, company F of the Second Texas Mounted Rifles manned Fort Lancaster from late 1861 to April of 1862. This company was W. P. Lane's Rangers. As late as 1867 Fort Lancaster was the site of a battle between Indians and the 9th[th] Cavalry.

Camp Melvin was more of a temporary post than Lancaster was. In fact it was an outpost of Fort Lancaster's situated on the Pecos River two miles west of the present-day State Highway 349 in northwestern Crockett County. Since this was the site of a pontoon crossing of the river, the crossing was more important than the military installation at that site. After opening in 1868, Camp Melvin had a post office for three years, and for the next thirteen years, stagecoaches made their stop at this point where a station was located.

In a short time, the military reduced the number of troops stationed at Camp Melvin, so Indians had their way with the stage. In 1873 thirteen Indians stole horses and mules belonging to the station and then killed Juan Chabavilla. The next year, Indians captured thirty-five horses belonging to the Torres ranch, which was near Camp Melvin. The raids continued and on June 27, 1878, five Indians attacked a stage traveling five miles beyond the crossing. One of the Indian's bullets injured a passenger. In the following years, this location carried the name Mail Station and later was called the Pontoon Crossing.

The visitor list at Camp Melvin not only included Indian raids but also outlaws. During the 1876-1877 time period, Jessie and Frank James made a visit to Camp Melvin. They owned a "Rest Ranch" within the surrounding area and stopped by to say hello. Their visit to Texas came shortly after they robbed a bank in Northfield, Minnesota.

As early as June 4, 1858, the army brass realized that the mail routes needed protection, so on this date the San Antonio-San Diego Mail received permission to build sheds at Fort Lancaster. These structures protected the mules and horses owned by the stage line.

By the fall of that same year, army officials had more orders for the troops at Fort Lancaster. They were to not only protect the mail line but also establish a picket at Escondido Springs for that purpose. This camp was 65 miles by stage northwest of Lancaster Crossing. Troops found themselves stretched over many miles of sagebrush and dry mesas as they watched for Indians who might attack the stage at any moment. In hopes of making travel conditions better, the army and stage line company worked together. They felt that the Lancaster Crossing needed a metal bridge, so it became a realty. Once in place, the bridge didn't enjoy very many years

Only the tall chimneys stand as reminders of the structures once called Fort Lancaster. Sharon Gentry views the hearth. Author's Collection

of use. Erosion by water and wind worked against the structure, which became impassable in a few years.

By 1859, all mail from San Antonio came over the Lower Trail, so the troops of Fort Lancaster were very important in protecting the stagecoaches. One of the most dangerous sections of the San Antonio-El Paso Mail Route was near Fort Lancaster. If the Indians didn't get you, lack of water might be the next culprit because drinking water was hard to find.

As travelers left Fort Lancaster traveling south, they hoped to make the

Escondido Water Hole and later Howard's Wells, also called Howard's Springs, for their next water stops.   Richard Austin Howard was a surveyor, scout, and soldier who worked in many areas of Texas. Most people think both Howard's Draw and Howard's Wells were named after him. Indian Chief, Big Ben, lead an attack on a government wagon train that had stopped at Howard's Wells on April 20, 1872. Many travelers were killed in the massacre including seventeen Mexican teamsters. The Indians took the mules the freighters had, and little is known about how much of the supplies were confiscated by the warriors.

In addition to Big Ben, one powerful Kiowa leader, Lone Wolf, participated in this fight. With his son Tau-ankia (Sit-in-the-saddle), Lone Wolf's men helped Big Ben fight off a patrol of the Ninth Cavalry who had ridden all the way from Fort Concho to protect this waterhole.

Some troopers may not have realized the influence that some of these Indians leaders had in their lifetime. Among the Indian chiefs who visited Washington D. C., one leader was named "Lone Wolf." This may or may not have been the same one who raided in West Texas. He went to Washington in one attempt to make peace, and he also met later with Custer, but the white man never could see things the way Lone Wolf did. In his later years, he realized the great White Father wouldn't listen to his brothers, so he fought the white man as much as he could.

Some time later, these same Indians engaged in a fight with Mackenzie at the North Fork of the Red River. Jose Carrion, while riding with the soldiers, recognized some forty-three mules owned by the Comanches as mules taken in the battle at Howard's Wells.

Since the Indian attacks continued in the Lancaster and Howard Wells area, the United States military decided they needed to establish another fort, which would protect the water source called Comanche Springs. A town called St. Gall appeared near the fort and was later known as Fort Stockton. This area was flat enough that early settlers dug irrigation ditches to channel water from the springs to surrounding fields.

Some men like Peter Gallagher envisioned a bigger town around the fort, so he purchased land for the town in 1868. He was ready for the influx of people.

St. Gall became a supply center for the army, the mail, wagon trains, and travelers. U. S. soldiers helped protect the stage coming in and out of Ft. Stockton. On October 13, 1869, Capt. Gamble of Fort Concho received a letter from Gen. Edward Donivan referring to a visit to some of his troops stationed at the Head of Middle Concho. One soldier out of the six living there had left to guard the stagecoach out of Fort Stockton.

In March of 1875, St. Gall became the county seat for Pecos County and included 1,100 people. Eventually, St. Gall changed its name to "Fort Stockton."

People who braved the elements to ride the stagecoaches often encountered a short food supply at the different stations. Col. E. V. Summer, Commander of the Department, sent messages to some quartermasters at the forts along the trail. He demanded that the posts provide the stage with supplies. This request hampered the soldiers at the post because they were also short of food supplies. At Fort Lancaster food was so scarce one time that stage passengers were fed from grain sacks intended for the mules.

Indians took all the mules from Fort Lancaster on one such raid, so the stage had no fresh mules to harness for the next relay. The same mules had to travel 20 more miles to the next station.

High water in the Sabinal and Nueces Rivers caused schedule problems in another area. One stage was known to arrive in San Antonio ten days late because of the swollen rivers. There was either too much water in the rivers or there wasn't enough water in the arid regions for the mules and horses to get a drink. Eighty percent of the time, the forts had to haul water at least 20 miles for their use.

Stage drivers made the long haul from Ft. Concho to Fort Stockton for several more years. When the stage left Fort Stockton, it headed westward toward Leon Springs, which was a very deep hole of water that was 30 feet wide. Many travelers wondered how deep the Leon Springs actually were. One time a company of cavalry decided to explore the pool. They tied all their ropes end to end to measure its depth, but they never reached the bottom of the spring. The stage also passed through Borilla Springs and El Merto on the way to Fort Davis. Probably the Indians such as Lone Wolf knew best of all where the watering holes were. Their lives depended on it.

Each watering hole was so important that different groups of people often

Lone Wolf, a Kiowa chief who lived in West Texas. Courtesy of the Heart of West Texas Museum, Colorado City, Texas.

gave a particular springs several different names. Leoncita Springs, on the San Antonio-El Paso Route, was located in Musquiz Canyon some 18.5 miles northeast of

Alpine. Presently Highway 118 drops into the canyon and passes by the remains of Manuel Musquiz's adobe structure.

Manuel started a ranch in this canyon southeast of Fort Davis. The Musquiz Creek rises nine miles south of Fort Davis and runs northeast for fifty-one miles. This creek passes through Musquiz Canyon so the stage passengers had a source of drinking water. Indians attacked the ranch during the Civil War, so Manuel finally fled to Mexico.

As late as 1907 there were some ruins of structures left at the old stage stop. Inquisitive visitors to the Musquiz property found an empty hole near a disintegrating casket and saw footprints of a man, a woman, and a child walking away from the hole. Some people thought there might have been a treasure buried there. Maybe some gold came by way of the stage. Other names for the same hole of water were Barrancas or Barnabas Springs. These names were found on very old maps.

While stagecoaches moved out of San Antonio on long roads to El Paso, a few coaches had shorter routes such as the one to Eagle Pass. Alex David opened this route from San Antonio to Eagle Pass around 1859. To make the business more lucrative, he obtained a mail route between the two towns and one from San Antonio to Bandera. He subcontracted the mail route to Mr. Santleban who lived near Castroville.

Some men got an early start as mail carriers, and August Santleban was such a young man. As a fourteen-year-old, his father directed him to carry the mail from his home four miles east of Castroville to Bandera and back. This ride was 64 miles round trip. Since the mail sack appeared at the Santleban house every Monday morning, August jumped on his horse at this time to make the run. The next day he returned with the mail and met the hack riding toward San Antonio. He completed his job when he turned over his mailbags to the driver.

The Civil War interrupted the mail business, so as a war veteran, August returned to the mail business in 1866 and won a contract to carry mail from San Antonio to Eagle Pass, and then to Fort Clark. By this time, the twenty-one year-old businessman was ready to make his own decisions without Dad. August rode one hundred sixty-two miles on a route that he had to make every six days. He purchased a three-seated hack for this venture and

Marker between Alpine and Fort Davis describing Manuel Musquiz's ranch.
Author's Collection.

charged twenty dollars for the trip. When he could, August made the stage trip as pleasant as possible. If he had several passengers and stopped at a station for the night where some people congregated, they joined in the activities. Sometimes they danced into the wee hours of the night.

Although this business provided August a chance to make money, he also had to be on the lookout for trouble, which came in at least two forms: the area was crawling with Indians as well as robbers called *ladrones*. The latter were Mexican men dressed in their silver-decorated costumes. They spoke with great politeness when meeting you, but all the time they had robbery in their mind. August started a stage line to Monterrey a year later with partner Adolph Muenzenberger, so he was even more apprehensive about these bandits who were so polite they never hurt anybody but successfully relieved many people of their valuables. August heard of one robbery where they held up a stage near Monterey in 1868. No one was hurt, but the *ladrones* stole ten thousand dollars.

That same year, August had a trying experience when he forded the swollen

Author Barbara Barton beside the ruins of the adobe Musquiz cabin in Musquiz Canyon.

Sabinas River on a tiny ferry-boat. The river was one hundred feet wide and fifteen feet deep, but August felt that his passengers needed to reach their destination of Monterrey; so he commenced to carry the mules and their harness in the first trip. The next trip included the coach and all the luggage, which made a heavy load. Each trip lasted about two hours, so the ferryman insisted that the passengers come along on this ride, but August refused.

Once the ferry was released from the bank, four ferrymen tried to guide it across the river with oars. The coach was top-heavy and the water was rough. Suddenly the ferry capsized and the stagecoach disappeared into the water. The ferrymen swam into the strong current and were able to get the ferry to right itself. The passengers, watching with horror on the bank, thought that all was lost including the driver.

Fortunately, August was a good swimmer so he made it to the bank, soaked but unharmed. Eventually, they used a rowboat to get the women and children safely across the river. Now August realized his predicament was serious because the passengers had no food or lodging for the night. To add to his problems he was about 50 miles from the next community.

A few Mexicans with their two-wheeled carts were also camped at the ferry that night. August inquired about something to eat and was able to buy food from them, but his campsite was pretty bleak that night with no bed or place for riders to sleep comfortably. The next day, men with about 30 carts rolled into the ferry area. August talked them into diving to find his stage. The men searched for the sunken stage, but three days elapsed before they were able to locate it downstream from the crossing. With ropes and pulleys, the men dragged the muddy coach from the river. All the luggage was in place as it was well tied to the top of the stag. After cleaning it the best he could, August paid the men and continued his trip.

Chapter 2: The Butterfield Stage Line

When the only stage line in Texas rambled from San Antonio to El Paso, John Butterfield brought hope of a new route crossing the Red river and moving toward the west. His success was connected to stagecoach builders in the eastern part of the country and what was happening to routes in that area.

The Butterfield Stage Line's success was probably the result of well-made coaches produced far away in the New England area. Although eastern stagecoach owners had their days of splendor, as their passengers bounced over the rough New England roads, their franchises existed for a rather short time. Any prolonged success in the stage business would have to be attributed largely to two craftsmen named Lewis Downing and J. Stephen Abbot.

In 1813 Lewis Downing built his first freight wagons, which were much in demand. His father-in-law drove stagecoaches at the time, so he influenced Lewis to look at another conveyance to build in his shop. Not much time passed before Lewis decided to make stagecoaches. The vehicles in use, which drove between nearby towns, were imported from England and had several problems.   Lewis thought he could make a better one.

The seats at the front and back of coaches made in Great Britain were narrow, so no one had very much legroom. In addition to the passengers feeling squeezed together, the driver sat cramped in a box on the outside of the coach. In 1826 Abbot, the designer, corrected many faults with his new version of the coach and Downing was exacting as he tended to the details. As a result of their efforts, Abbot and Downing were very successful in making coaches. They sold their improved coaches in Europe, Canada, Australia, Africa, South America, and Mexico.

The two craftsmen made many changes to the old coach that was first in use. They widened the ends enough to seat three people on both benches. On the top of the coach, they built rails around the edges so that the driver could place as much as 100 pounds of express up there and still have room for three people to sit behind him. Instead of the driver sitting in a box, they extended the seat to reach the full width of the coach.

With this arrangement, two passengers could sit beside the driver. These places to sit on top of the stage were much in demand by passengers, but the driver always determined who could climb on top with him. Sometimes a congressman rode the stage, and if the weather were nice, the driver would invite his special guest to sit with him. Other passengers noticed that the driver particularly liked to pick a pretty lady to sit beside him on the journey.

The egg shape of a stagecoach allowed the vehicle to support more than 100 times its own weight. Since a six or eight-ply belt of four-inch wide bull-hide leather formed the brace, the coach moved with a rocking-chair action.

The stage wheels always presented a problem to the owners. They were made of wood incased in an iron rim. If it rained on the wheels, the wood expanded so that the driver watched it bulge over the rim. On dry, hot days, the temperature caused the wood to shrink. If this happened a driver feared that the wooden wheel would separate from the metal rim.

By 1840, the stages were few and far between in the eastern states. Most owners of stage lines looked for other markets and realized they owned something that nobody wanted. Just as their despair increased, gold miners seeking California's riches brought a new destination to the transportation companies. The goal of hundreds of men in 1848 was to leave the eastern states and reach California so they could become rich. Stagecoach owners pricked up their ears and listened. They had a new market, a new destination, and the mail lines figured into this new venture.

In 1857 Congress authorized the delivery of mail to California twice weekly on a type of transportation that would carry passengers as well as mail. They stipulated that a person would be able to make the trip from St. Louis to San Francisco in twenty-five days. Across Texas, this route traversed the Red River near Gainsville, and passed through Fort Belknap, Camp Cooper, Fort Griffin, crossed the North Concho River near Carlsbad, went to Camp Charlotte, Centralia Draw, Castle Gap, Pine Springs (the Pinery in Guadalupe Mountains,) into New Mexico and finally to Fort Franklin near El Paso.

Congress declared that the lowest bidder would win the contract. Although bids came flowing in, much controversy made it hard to decide the true winner. Finally, John Butterfield won against the competition with his bid of $600,000. The fact that Butterfield was a longtime friend of Pres. James Buchanan may or may not have influenced this decision.

John Butterfield was an ambitious lad who dreamed of driving stagecoaches while he was still very young. At the age of nineteen, his dream came true, and he spent the next thirty years involved with the business. In 1850 Butterfield convinced Wells and Fargo both to merge with him, and the three men formed the American Express Company. Seven years later Butterfield won a million-dollar contract to start the Butterfield Mail Route in one year. His group had twelve months to prepare the 2,700 miles of fair to primitive roads. They had to build stations, hire drivers, as well as buy supplies and livestock.

To develop the stage line from St. Louis to San Francisco was a massive undertaking. They purchased 250 stagecoaches, built 139 relay stations, employed over 800 people, and bought 1,800 head of livestock. Butterfield's Company had to build a station every twenty miles as well as drill a water well in many cases to insure an adequate water supply.

Conditions for passengers riding the wagons were almost intolerable. Later some passengers said the stations were downright crude. In fact, the ground outside was said to be cleaner than the floors inside many of the stations. Passengers never got to sleep in a bed, so their naps, taken while sitting upright in the stagecoach, were often interrupted. They also suffered from the heat and dust. After riding the stage for a week, most passengers learned to sleep while sitting next to other passengers and parcels. Food was also very sparse. Passengers complained of being served wormy crackers, jerky cooked over cowchips, or other meat as tough as a mule.

There were nine divisions on this route, which included from St. Louis to Tipton Missouri; to Ft. Smith, Arkansas; to Colbert Ferry crossing on the Red River; to Fort Chadbourne; to Franklin (El Paso); to Ft. Yuma, Arizona; to Los Angeles; and on to San Francisco.

Everyone, including Butterfield, was pleased to see the stage embark on its maiden journey from St. Louis September 15, 1858 within the specified time. Sometimes it got behind its schedule and other times the stage surprised everybody by getting ahead. As the stage neared Fort Phantom Hill on its first trip, the driver saw a row of rock stables and anticipated a change of horses. Much to his dismay, the stage company failed to bring a fresh team to this stop, so he and the horses labored on toward Fort Chadbourne.

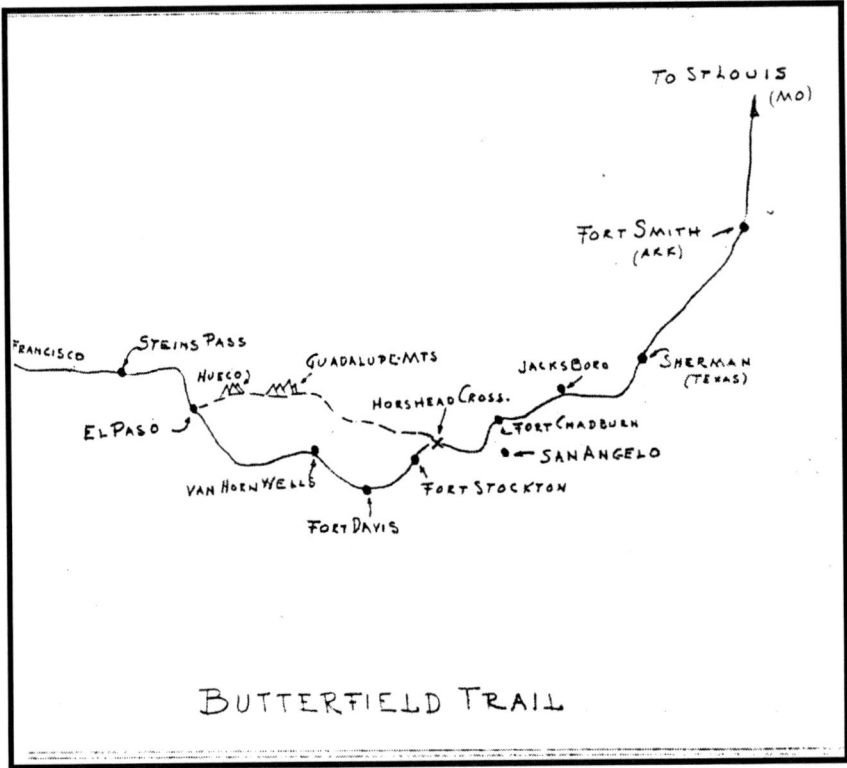

The Butterfield Mail Route, started in 1857, began in St. Louis and ended in San Francisco.

The troops and families at Fort Chadbourne welcomed the first official trip of the mail, for this fort was very young and the troops had very little entertainment headed their way. Some of the soldiers lived in tents with their fellow comrades, while others lived in the rock barracks. Any diversion from the norm was good for the soldier's moral.

The driver, equally glad, saw a team of Spanish mules in a nearby corral. Unknown to him, these mules were wild. It took several hours to catch and hitch them to the stage wagon. With passengers loaded, the driver popped the whip to start the team to the next station. The mules had other ideas as they pitched and twisted the harness into a frightening mess.

As they bucked and fought the driver's attempts to rein them in, supplies fell off the stage so that the prairie around them was decorated with the mail and suitcases. Much later the driver straightened the lines, reloaded the items, and pointed the team toward Grape Creek, some twenty-two miles away. The Fort Chadbourne soldiers had to return to their duties as the stage rolled over the nearby hill toward the next station.

There is uncertainty among writers as to whether the next station was in northwest Coke County, or could it have been on Yellow Wolf Creek, which was then called Grape Creek? This second location was sixteen miles west of Fort Chadbourne. The most accepted position for the Grape Creek Station according to historians was a point on the North Concho a mile or two south of present day Carlsbad.

In 1861 the Butterfield Line had been in business some time, and the Grape Creek Station personnel included keeper Joel Pennington, his wife, his brother-in-law Charles Cox and the hostler Elijah Helms. On a fateful day in February of 1861, thirty

Stagecoach at Fort Chadbourne. G. P. Crutchfield built this replica of the Butterfield Stagecoach for the annual play, "The Albany Fandangle." Picture by the author.

Comanche warriors attacked the station. After rounding up all the stock that the Penningtons had, the arrogant chief told the family that unless they got a better grade of livestock, he would return in a month and kill them.

By the time the chief had returned, the Butterfield had shut down operations. All the Penningtons owned was a wagon team and one or two ponies. This fact caused the chief to attack the house with intent to kill them. The station in which the people were hiding was sturdy as it was made of split logs. After trying to shoot their way into the house without any success, the Comanches decided to set the station on fire. Pennington ran from the house and received a blast from an Indian rifle that tore part of his face off. Helms and Cox drove the Indians away and hid Pennington in some bushes. Helms quickly rode to Fort Chadbourne for help. Surprising to most witnesses, Pennington lived over the wounds and terrible ordeal.

After the stage left the Grape Creek station, the next stop was some thirty miles down the road at the Carlsbad Station. Most historians agree that this location was the same place on the North Concho River as Camp Johnston had been located only six years before. This fort was always a tent city that moved wherever water was located. The soldiers at Camp Johnston had been given their instructions to move to Fort Chadbourne in 1852.

From Carlsbad, the stagecoach had a stop on Dry Creek, (some sources call this West Rocky Creek) not far from the Arden community; then it ambled on westward. It is believed that this station moved four miles westward in Section 59, Block 10 of the Houston and Texas Central Railway Co. survey and became known as Johnson Station.

When the flood of 1882 washed away the former county seat town of Ben Ficklin, the water-stained pages of Tom Green County Probate Minutes, Ms. – County Clerks Office, volume "A" was rescued. This volume substantiates this move.

About the time of the Butterfield Trail's existence, another stage road called the Immigrant Trail came from San Antonio. It passed through Fredericksburg, to the head of the Concho River and crossed the Butterfield Trail near the location of Arden, Texas. Claude Hudspeth, a Texas historian, says there is a stage station made of adobe near the point where the present-day road turns away from Arden and goes south toward Sherwood.

This location would be on the north side of the Middle Concho. The Butterfield Trail was on the northeast side of the river. The Immigrant Trail included Horsehead Crossing as it angled westward toward Ft. Sumner, New Mexico.

As the Butterfield route left the Arden area, it passed along the Middle Concho River at the point where Kiowa Creek flowed into it on the stage's voyage through West Texas. This meeting of the two rivers was about 18 miles west of Sherwood, Texas. The stage line driving this route was part of the Coughlin Stage Company. Horses were changed at Camp Charlotte, which came into existence April 1858, near this location. From 1857 until 1869 the Overland Mail traveled through this point, and it was a stage stop rather than a post office at this time.

Capt. G. G. Huntt, 4th U. S. Cavalry, was commander of Fort Concho. On December 27, 1867, he wrote a letter to his superior reporting a scouting trip he made near Camp Charlotte. Since this time is shortly after the Civil War, it is not clear whether any soldiers had returned to Camp Charlotte at this time or not. Someone in the area told Capt. Huntt about civilians' bodies that were found in a wash along the bank of the river, plus another body about fifty paces away from the stream.

Paper money was scattered all about the area. This fact and the way one man's body showed signs of torture, charred and blackened spots on his body, told the troopers that the Indians did the job. From papers on the corpses, the soldiers identified the bodies. They were James and John Ketchum, Robert Correpossa, William Truman, and Thomas Donnell. The soldiers determined from the papers that James Ketchum sold cattle in New Mexico and was returning to his home in San Saba by way of the Middle Concho. One of Capt. Huntt's men, Price Cooper, had his home in San Saba, so he agreed to return the money to Ketchum's family.

Capt. Huntt knew that he should try to catch the Indians who did this horrible deed, so he followed the Indian trail with seven men as they rode 130 miles from Fort Concho. They were always about a day behind the warriors as they located smoldering campfires but never found the Indians.

Another member of the Ketchum family, Black Jack (Tom), came to this area in 1880 with his older brothers, Berry and Sam. Before Camp Charlotte closed, outlaw Black Jack spent some time among the hills of that same area. He had one or two caves situated high enough on their slopes to see the area below him. Tom chose to rob trains and banks, so he left the Butterfield coaches alone.

The Civil War brought an abrupt stop to many mail routes because most of

The site of Coughlin's Stage Stand near Camp Charlotte. Author's Collection.
The soldiers abandoned the forts to fight in the war. Since the stages had no protection from the Indians, drivers were afraid to make their runs through unprotected regions.

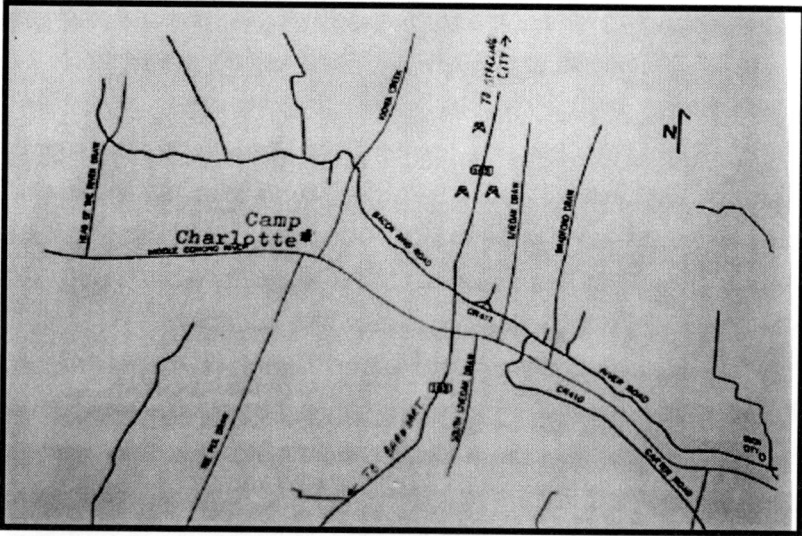

Map showing Camp Charlotte west of the highway connecting Sterling City to Barnhart, Texas. The Stage line moved from east to west on this map. Map courtesy of Joyce Gray.

In 1867 soldiers reoccupied many of the forts and camps along the Butterfield Trail. However, Fort Chadbourne and Fort Belknap were abandoned permanently because of the lack of water. Fort Concho, built in 1867, and Fort Griffin were established after the Civil War.

By 1880, the Camp Charlotte stage stop and fort were listed on the U. S. Census. At that time, the camp was home to 13 soldiers, one blacksmith, one surgeon, one laborer, and three stage drivers. These men who drove their teams daily through West Texas included Allen Harris, a 25-year old white male born in Louisiana; John D. Anders, a 24 year-old Texan; and Jerome Hardin, a 21 year-old man born in Indiana. Most of the soldiers who bunked at Camp Charlotte were black men, buffalo soldiers. Their ages ranged from 21 to 34.

They had a frustrating time protecting the mail route because the U. S. government sent infantry soldiers instead of cavalry to this remote location. This situation meant that the soldiers could not mount a horse to chase the enemy, so they defended the fort but little else.

Camp Charlotte may have been a supply depot for Fort Concho and other subposts because a road connected it to Colorado City, which was the nearest T & P. Railroad station established in 1881.

By 1885, settlers formed a town of Camp Charlotte, and the second post office for this camp was built inside the nearby Burris Store. Up to this time, the Overland Mail left the letters at the fort. On November 6, 1885, William Garrison took over as postmaster. This little community had a post office until March 9, 1889, at which time the mail was left in San Angelo, some forty miles away.

Many years later when the camp was inactive, a committee of women decided the location of the old camp needed a marker. The members of the Pocahontas Chapter of Daughters of the American Revolution of San Angelo erected the marker November 2, 1934. Mr. and Mrs. Fayette Tankersley, along with their daughter Verda, directed Mrs. W. M. Tolson, Mrs. H. B. Cox, Mrs. V. G. Holland, and Mrs. Sam Jones to the site. Since the Fayette Tankersleys lived near Camp Charlotte during their early married life, this visit to the area was like a homecoming to them and a chance to relive memories of the Concho River.

Fayette remembered driving cattle along the Butterfield Trail with his father when he was 12 years old. This first trip took place in 1871 as they herded cattle to Mexico. Fayette said that he had made the trip many times since his initial ride. Old timers described the trips in the Butterfield Stage as down right scary. They explained that if the coach had few passengers inside, the riders would bump from side to side as they grasped for any object with which to anchor themselves. The curtains flapped in the breeze and rainwater drained through the curtains onto the passengers.

When the Conklin Stage riders saw Camp Charlotte for the first time, the soldiers lived in tents and the horses, as well as mules, were enclosed in a pen made of piled brush. The mules proved hard to catch out of this pen also, but the first trip through Camp Charlotte ended with the stage leaving the soldiers and taking some spare mules with them.

In 1858, the stage route left Camp Charlotte and traveled to the Head of the Concho River Station and passed the tributaries of the Centralia Draw as it bounced along the northwestern side of future Reagan County. According to the U. S. Postal Department, the Centralia Station was not one of the stops on the first trip. Later such a station was made at the Centralia water hole below the Stiles community. Centralia Station, some ten or twelve miles west of Stiles had the last water for the stage riders and horses before making the long trip through desolate countryside to Castle Gap.

By 1889, the James Belcher family lived on the south bank of Centralia Draw at the site of the Butterfield station ruins. Water provided at this stop was stored in a cistern. This structure allowed the water to seep into the storage container from an underground spring.

As the stage routes moved about in West Texas after the Civil War, the routes often changed so the stage could stop at the point where water was most likely to be found. Old timers point to several different crossings sited on the Centralia. Weather conditions and amount of water available seemed to determine which crossing was used.

This stretch of the trail passed through the Castle Mountains whose rim rock looked similar to the parapets of a medieval castle. People traveling on the stage at this location were between the present-day towns of Crane and McCamey. The Gap is a mile long but only yards wide at its narrowest point, so the stage driver had to be on the lookout for Indian attacks.

As the stagecoach passed through the gap, Castle Mountain's summit reared up on the north side and King Mountain created the southern barrier. From the flat plains the passengers rode through previously, these elevations of 3,141 feet must have seemed gigantic.

The Castle Gap stage stop at the west end of the Gap was a welcomed site. At this location, travelers climbed out of the stage and walked into a two-storied building made of native stone. Travelers, as well as the horses, could enjoy nearby spring water on this route, which Indians called Weich Pah, "Gap Water."

Indians frequented the Gap as they moved to and from the Edwards Plateau on the eastern side where they hunted buffalo. They also collected salt at Juan Cordona Lake some fifteen miles west of the Gap.

Castle Gap witnessed many catastrophes and many hidden treasures are said to be in that area. Outlaws and Indians roamed these greasewood plains in the 1800s. The forty-niners traveling back to Texas supposedly left a horseshoe keg of gold in the area. In 1860, treasure from the Butterfield stage was hidden. Outlaws stashed away gold they commandeered, and Emperor Maximillan's treasures were left here in 1867. Before Horsehead Crossing was used, travelers spying the Pecos River stayed on its east bank and traveled along its path northwest to Pope's Camp, which was near the New Mexico border. From this point, the stage made its way to El Paso.

Soon the trail was changed so that wagons and stages used the famous Horsehead Crossing on the Pecos because it was the only place along the river where the banks were flat enough for travelers to make it to the water's edge. This ford was only twelve miles west by southwest from the Castle Gap area. This crossing on the Pecos River is near present Farm Road 11 and is situated 12 miles northwest of Girvin, Texas. This crossing was so named due to the many skeletons of horses and mules that died nearby. Their death, brought about by drinking the briny river water or wading in the quicksand near the crossing, caused many ranchers and citizens of the area to dread this ford.

In later years, stages left this route at Gap Rock Ridge as they went east, followed the Pecos along its eastern side to a gap that was seven or eight miles northwest of the present Texon Oil Field. From this point, the stage drivers traveled over the ridge to Sweet Gum flat in Upton County and came around the small hills near Rankin. From this point, the stages angled southwest to go around King's Mountain through present day McCamey and on to the Pontoon River Crossing, which was about 25 miles below Horsehead Crossing.

By 1860 the Texas Legislature tried to intervene in the mail routes by passing two bills that would fund a toll bridge over the Pecos River. They thought these funds could be used to improve the route. One bridge was to be at Horsehead Crossing and the other was located near Fort Lancaster where the San Antonio-San Diego line crossed. Such a good idea had a terrible demise. The Civil War put a temporary end to the stage lines as manpower was needed elsewhere. Also the Indians took back the country where stages once rolled.

There has been some discussion through the years as to whether there ever was a stage station at Horsehead Crossing. So many bones graced the area from dead horses and cattle that most people thought there never was a station. However, some researchers have found remains of adobe walls near the crossing, which indicates that someone may have run the station for a while.

Henry Skillman became more or less famous for being the first stage driver to leave Horsehead Crossing on a Sunday morning and bring his charges into El Paso for the first arrival of the Overland Stage to that town in the predawn hours of September 30, 1858. Skillman managed this feat by driving ninety-six hours with no rest or relief. His many experiences leading up to this day prepared him as best as any could.

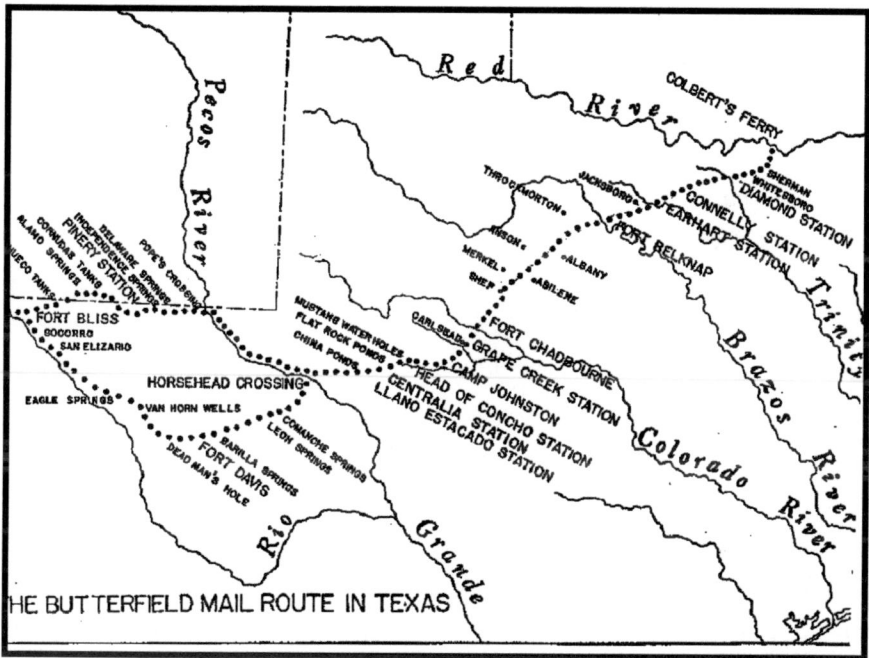

THE BUTTERFIELD MAIL ROUTE IN TEXAS

After several years of freighting, Skillman Skillman started managing the mail as a horseback carrier between San Antonio and El Paso in 1849 and 1850. The following year he received an official contract to deliver U. S. mail on this route. By 1852 Skillman drove the first monthly run of a Concord stage pulled by six mules along the same route. As many as 18 soldiers accompanied him in his first voyages over the Indian infested plains. The stage eventually changed to a freight wagon because there was more demand for him to carry goods than people. After several years of freighting, Skillman advertised that he would take passengers over the San Antonio-Santa Fe trip in a canvas-topped wagon for $25. This trip would be a grueling nineteen-day affair. Much to Skillman's dismay, his passenger-hauling was not successful, so he lost his contract to David Wasson. Although Skillman thought his stage driving was over by 1854, the new Butterfield Overland Trail activated him once more.

When drivers like Skillman drove along the Pecos River, they often met trail drives. Cattle herds of Loving, Goodnight, and Chisum used the Horsehead Crossing even though it was dangerous. The Butterfield Overland Mail route entered Culberson County from the east. It crossed the Rustler Hills, followed the Delaware River west near the New Mexican-Texas border, and had a stage stop along this river for the weary travelers. This location is on the Kowden Ranch, a place about 20 miles east of the Pinery. The next few miles on the trail climbed upward toward the Guadalupe Mountains. The Pinery at Pine Springs was a stage stop in the Guadalupes, built in 1858.

The Pinery, known as a place to cross the Guadalupe Pass, had visitors like Lt. Francis T. Bryan and Capt. Randolph B. Marcy in 1849, years before stagecoaches were in West Texas. By 1850 John Russell Barlett camped at the springs called the Pinery. Capt. John Pope visited this waterhole in 1854.

None of these visitors were more excited about the beautiful mountains and cool water from Pine Springs than those making the first westbound trip by stage on September 28, 1858. Henry Ramstein and his helpers lived in tents and a recently made corral of pine logs held the horses needed on the next leg of the journey. This stop called The Pinery received its name from the clumps of trees growing nearby. The Ramsteins fed the travelers venison and baked beans until they had to resume their ride.

The next leg of travel was rough as the passengers in the stage jolted down the pass trail. At the foot of the mountain, they met an eastbound stage. The groups exchanged experiences and for a moment the 2,800 miles of the trail were connected by the two stages.

The Ramsteins intended for this location to be a permanent stop, so within two months they erected a high-walled rock fence for protection. The construction was of limestone slabs and adobe arranged so that the walls were 30 inches thick and 11 feet tall. This corral looked like a fort because it had only one entrance and inside the walls, Ramstein made three rooms with mud roofs.

The builders thought of everything as they channeled water from the springs into the fort by way of a ditch and stored it in a tank. Inside the rock walls was housed a wagon repair shop as well as a blacksmith's forge. This stage stop had a lot of activity, so Henry Ramstein hired six to eight helpers. At this stop, workers had to be prepared for the arrival of the stage four times a week. When they were not helping the visitors, men hauled water to other stops along the way at stations that had none.

When any news of Indian movement reached the Pinery, the men brought livestock and people inside their fortress for protection. Although they never lost a

Ruins of the Pinery Stage Station in the Guadalupe Mountains. Photo courtesy of Bob Tate.

person at this stop, news traveling from other stage stops was not so good. At a mail station in Arizona, three men were killed. The deceased had previously been workers helping to build the Pinery. An Apache attack in Arizona also stopped the mail service.

The Pinery had another kind of tragedy. Stage line owners decided to close this station eleven months after it opened because Indian danger was too great, and Ft. Davis wanted mail delivered in their direction. The following year, the Overland

Mail Route shifted south so that Forts Stockton and Davis could protect the stage lines. Structures built at the Pinery remained, so when the Mecalero Indians were no longer a threat, the station was used by freighters and soldiers for shelter.

A stage stop south of the Guadalupes diverted the mail coach to flatter ground. Leaving this station, the mail stopped at a few more springs on the way to El Paso; the Crow Springs and the Hueco Tank. From this last stop, the stage made its way to Franklin, later called El Paso.

Many men who were forced to ride the stages of West Texas noticed there was quite a difference in these conveyances and the ones they were used to riding in the eastern United States. One big difference was the availability of trained horses and mules to pull the stages. Capt. R. G. Carter described the wild mules he witnessed at various stage stops in West Texas. He said the mules were brought out of their pens blindfolded. The passengers as well as the driver got in their seats before these animals were harnessed to the stage. The driver grabbed his reins, gave the signal to remove the blinders and lunged forward as the mules and stage made their run to the next station.

Carter said that although the route was driven tri-weekly, mail might make it to their post where he was stationed only once a month if the rivers were full of rainwater. If rain stopped the stages, men mounted on horses brought the mail through the mud and high water using mail pouches on their saddles.

Most days in West Texas were dry and hot, even droughty, so the mail had no problem at this time except stage drivers had to find drinking water. One important town on the Butterfield Trail became Fort Stockton. The Fort provided the needed troops because several mail routes passed through their town. Another positive factor was the Comanche Springs near the fort. They provided much needed water for the horses and mules, as well as the travelers. Soldiers at Fort Stockton might see travelers coming to town in the Butterfield Overland Stage or in one of the hacks driven over the upper and lower San Antonio-El Paso-San Diego roads. Their town was a cross-roads for many travelers.

John Lackey drove the stage as it made this daring trip from Fort Concho to El Paso. Lackey started his job in 1868, a time when he and his brothers were settling into their new home in Sherwood, Texas, about 25 miles southwest of Fort Concho.

The Civil War left the Lackeys of Kentucky without anything. Their livelihood had been that of riverboat builders, which was done with slave labor. Now that the Lackeys no longer could build boats, they came to Texas. John brought his brothers Charles and Williams along with him. John stayed with the stagecoach until he returned to Kentucky in 1872 to marry Mary Elizabeth Tomblin. When they moved to San Angelo, John left the stage driving and won the job of county clerk for the new county of Tom Green.

While the Butterfield Stage Line was in its glory days, its owner thought that these stages could go faster than any other conveyance on earth. Butterfield was particularly fond of his Texas mules. Captain Harrison owned and piloted a 20,000-ton steamboat, which he raved about as much as Butterfield did about his mules. The boat was 679 feet long and in 1858, it was considered an enormous ship with 7,000 yards of sail and eight engines producing 11,000 horsepower. Harrison bet Butterfield that he could pilot his boat from New York around Cape Horn to San Francisco faster than Butterfield's mules could take the stage from St. Louis to San Francisco.

The Great Western, built by Isambard Brunel and launched in 1837, was a steamer driven by paddles. It left Great Britian in April of 1838 to cross the Atlantic to America the first time.

Butterfield thought his stages were faster so the bet was on between a horse or mule-driven coach and a ship.

Butterfield prepared his coaches and his livestock. He spent nearly $50,000 for new equipment. Excitement about the race spilled over into every stage stop. Each employee tried to prepare teams of horses or mules and equipment for the race in such as way as to make them successful.

On the appointed day for the race to begin, the steamer left New York March 10, 1858. By the rules of the race, the stage left St. Louis four days later, on March 14, 1858. Townspeople, as well as those in the country, waved at the stage as it passed them. The drivers received cheers as they crossed Texas, New Mexico, and Arizona.

Each stage driver made a mighty effort, and when the dust cleared in San Francisco, everybody knew the stage made the 3,000-mile trip in 20 days. The Great Western steamer pulled into port 36 hours later. Butterfield won the $100,000 prize.

By 1860, the Butterfield Overland Mail looked like a success story with the postage rate easing to ten cents per half ounce. For the year 1860, receipts totaled $119,766.77. Sherman, Texas, became a distribution point for all mail in the state. At that time the Concord stage not only carried mail, but they also received revenue from five or six passengers. Their fee averaged $200 for a one-way ticket the full distance. Most travelers tried to remain on the coach for the duration of their trip. Otherwise, another traveler might get their seat. If this happened, the stranded person might have to wait weeks for another ride to become available.

When the stage left Fort Stockton, its next destinations were Leon Hole, Hackberry Hole, Barrila Springs, Limpia, and then Fort Davis. No true rivers flowed at these stops until they reached Limpia Creek on their last leg to the fort.

Between Fort Davis and Ft. Quitman lay another barren stretch. The stage stopped at Barrel Springs, Deadman Hole, and Van Horn Springs on the way. James Hudson Van Horn commanded the 8th[th] Infantry, which camped at the Van Horn Springs.

At this point, the stage business was very successful. However, the Civil War dealt the owners a real blow because they no longer had soldier protection against the Indians and outlaws. Butterfield sold his interest in the line, and it was eventually moved northward out of the state of Texas. Mail traveling by trains also affected the need for stages.

Eli Bates holds the reins as F. C. Taylor sits beside him. They are leaving the town of Ben Ficklin in 1879 on the San Antonio-El Paso route. Passenger Ada Clapp was the daughter of the coach maker. F. C. Taylor managed this route long after the Butterfield stages left Texas. Courtesy of the Tom Green County Historical Society.

The stage business continued after the Civil War, but the names of many businesses changed. A stage running from Fort Concho to Fort Davis was owned by the Texas and California Stage Company. By the year 1887, shipping individual articles over the stage required the company's Way Bill. Such a Way Bill written September 7, 1887, shows the stage leaving Fort Concho with a destination of Fort Davis. The coach brought two sacks and left with two sacks, which the drivers listed as Bobos. The freight list included one buffalo robe consigned by L. S. Hart with destination of El Paso because it was left behind at the last stop. A lady from Fort Stockton was to receive a sack on this trip for the same reason; she left it at the last stop.

This "Way Bill" reminded drivers that each package and each person on the stage was their responsibility. Agents were to examine the Freight List and take charge of the freight when received. They allowed each passenger 40 pounds of luggage. If their valises were in excess of that amount, it would be charged as freight. One of the more interesting statements on the Way Bill said, "Dogs are not allowed to be carried on the Stages at any pricc."

While the Butterfield Stage Line disappeared, new stage managers appeared in West Texas to set up their headquarters on the Concho River.

Fayette Tankersley remembered driving cattle up the Butterfield Trail as a young man. Many years later, he helped put a marker on the stage line that passed near his home in Irion County. Photo is courtesy of the Irion County Historical Society.

Chapter 3: From Fort Concho Westward

When Capt. George G. Huntt halted his Fourth U. S. Cavalry where the North and Main Concho rivers met on the plains of West Texas, he saw no stagecoaches. That December day in 1867 marked the beginning of a military camp called Camp Hatch. Some of the soldiers named it Tent City since that's what they lived in for a while, but eventually it took on a different appearance.

When given the permanent name "Fort Concho," it slowly evolved into a beautiful post where quarried limestone officer quarters and barracks lined the parade ground. The first visitors they had to their fort area were a few ranchers and quite a number of buffalo hunters who piled their hides nearby in huge stacks.

But quickly the scene changed as a combination of saloon owners, prostitutes, and gamblers moved in to grab a share of the soldiers' pay. They established themselves on the north side of the river, opposite the fort on the south bank. Eventually banks and stores made their presence known to the growing community. Wagon Yards provided the "hotels" for most travelers to this new burg called San Angela.

Visitors who entered the saloons encountered a frightening situation. With guns blazing between drunken gamblers and other patrons, this area of town became so dangerous with frequent killings that an officer from Fort Concho said, "I wouldn't leave the fort after dark."

A few miles south of the fort another community, called Ben Ficklin, emerged the same year, 1867. Mr. Ficklin, its namesake, decided to develop a stage station there. Benjamin F. Ficklin, a man of Pony Express fame, came to Texas to involve himself with the stagecoach business in 1861. Ficklin had excellent credentials in the business world. From the time he graduated from Virginian Military Institute, several southern businessmen called on him to make trips to England as their purchasing agent.

Years earlier he had directed successful stage lines in Alabama, so building a business in Texas was a natural step for Ben Ficklin. In the summer of 1867, Ficklin and his friend Frederick Sawyer purchased a mail route from Fort Smith, Arkansas, to San Antonio. From this hub city, they developed an additional line to El Paso. Ben Ficklin's brother, Slaughter, joined him eventually as the two built a stage station near the newly organized Fort Concho. By January 30, 1869, Ficklin owned 640 acres on the south side of the South Concho River in a spot that was seven miles from the fort.

From this location, the stage owner handled large government mail routes from Austin and San Antonio to El Paso. His good friends, Francis Corbett and F. C. Taylor, who once worked with him in Alabama agreed to help with this Texas venture. Living in San Antonio appealed to Ficklin much more than pitching his tent in the wilds of West Texas, but he realized that he had better live nearer the action. His money was invested in the stage line, so it was his first priority.

Ben Ficklin named his operation the Concho Mail Station. His most important structure to build was the eight-feet high corral for the stage horses. Indians regularly raided any pen full of horses, so Ficklin lined the inside of the corral with heavy posts standing upright, anchored firmly in the ground. Between these posts, he ran a chain so the animals could not flee over or under the chain. His large adobe station had a kitchen and commissary for the travelers, as well as shops to repair wagons, harnesses, and wheels.

Other buildings housed the workers and protected the coaches. Racing greyhound dogs was another passion of Ben Ficklin's, so behind the corral he built a dog kennel. This impressive structure was 200 feet long, big enough to house fifty dogs. When visiting politicians or other dignitaries came through the Ficklin Stage Stop, Ben entertained them with a dog race. Travelers on the El Paso-San Antonio stage ate a meal at Ben Ficklin's Concho stop for 50 cents. It did not include any perishable food such as butter or fresh vegetables.

But the employees of the stage stand kept the cooks well supplied with plenty buffalo and venison meat. Stage passengers paid $75 in gold to ride the stage from El Paso to San Antonio. Drivers needed a little more than 48 hours to push the stage from San Antonio to Ft. Concho, a trip that covered over 200 miles and cost $25.

The town of Ben Ficklin that was built around the stage stop was a bit more peaceful than the wild San Angela. Soon it had mercantile stores and churches; it was a place where officers and their wives enjoyed shopping and visiting. One of the stage lines moving in and out of San Angelo at a regular clip was the line to Knickerbocker and points southwestward, which finally ended in Comstock's stage stop some 160 miles away. Such a drive was hot and dusty during the summer months but cold and winterish at other times.

After the Flood of 1882, much of Ben Ficklin was demolished, so Saint Angela developed successful businesses, more wagon yards, and churches. As the town, now named San Angelo, grew across the river from Fort Concho, people needed

Benjamin F. Ficklin. Noted Plainsman.

Ben Ficklin set up a successful stagecoach business several miles from Fort Concho. Courtesy of the West Texas Collection, Angelo State University.

transportation. Indians and outlaws knew the stage route almost as well as the drivers did, and they often challenged the stage-hands to a life-threatening race. Although the lengthy drive from San Angelo to Comstock was hard on the most strong-willed stage driver, several stout-hearted men tackled the job. In 1902 Ralph Watson did not know that he was making a longtime commitment to stage lines when he drove this route for Jess Moore and W. J. Ellis the first time.

Watson came to the Ozona area in 1902 and taught the three R's in the nearby schoolhouse. Since Watson had college credits from Howard Payne, he was in demand as an educator. Ralph Watson had the respect of the community, and at the end of the day teaching, he could go home to a nice meal and comfortable bed. Watson held classes on the Whitehead Ranch and later in the Crockett County School. But Watson traded this calm life for one with much more adventure: he loved animals, and the great outdoors beckoned to him so much that he traded the classroom for the open prairies. Soon the teacher drove stagecoaches.

His life changed drastically. Whereas school children could stay in their seats and obey his instructions, some of those wild horses hooked to the stage had other plans. If they could buck and tumble the stagecoach over, their life would be easier, they thought.

Other times Watson felt the bitter north winds blowing on him or stuck his coach in a muddy road. During those times, he surely had flashbacks as to how calm the classroom was.

The following year, W. E. Newton also handled the mail hack from San Angelo to Comstock. This mail and passenger line rolled across the dusty trails of West Texas and through lonesome prairies. During the 1903 to 1905 time period, Newton drove as well as owned this mail contract with Albert Kincaid, his partner. Newton said that when he left Ft. Concho, passed through Knickerbocker, and headed to Sherwood, he usually met another hack of his bringing the mail toward the fort.

This route was called a star route. That name meant that mail contracts were low and expenses were high. The owners hoped for passengers and express to put their ledger in the black. Stage horses were changed every 20 miles, so for this 160-mile run to Comstock, Kincaid owned about 100 horses.

Harnesses were another important item for the stage line, but these various sizes of leather straps had a way of breaking at the worst times. Arthur Williams and his brother had a shop in Ozona where they mended leather, so their work was in demand. V. I. Pierce, in his book *Yesteryear,* said that the Williams brothers worked

Stage Route from Fort Concho to Ozona

X Fort Concho

Sherwood X   X

Knickerbocker

X Monument

BarnhartX

X Highlonesome

X Ozona

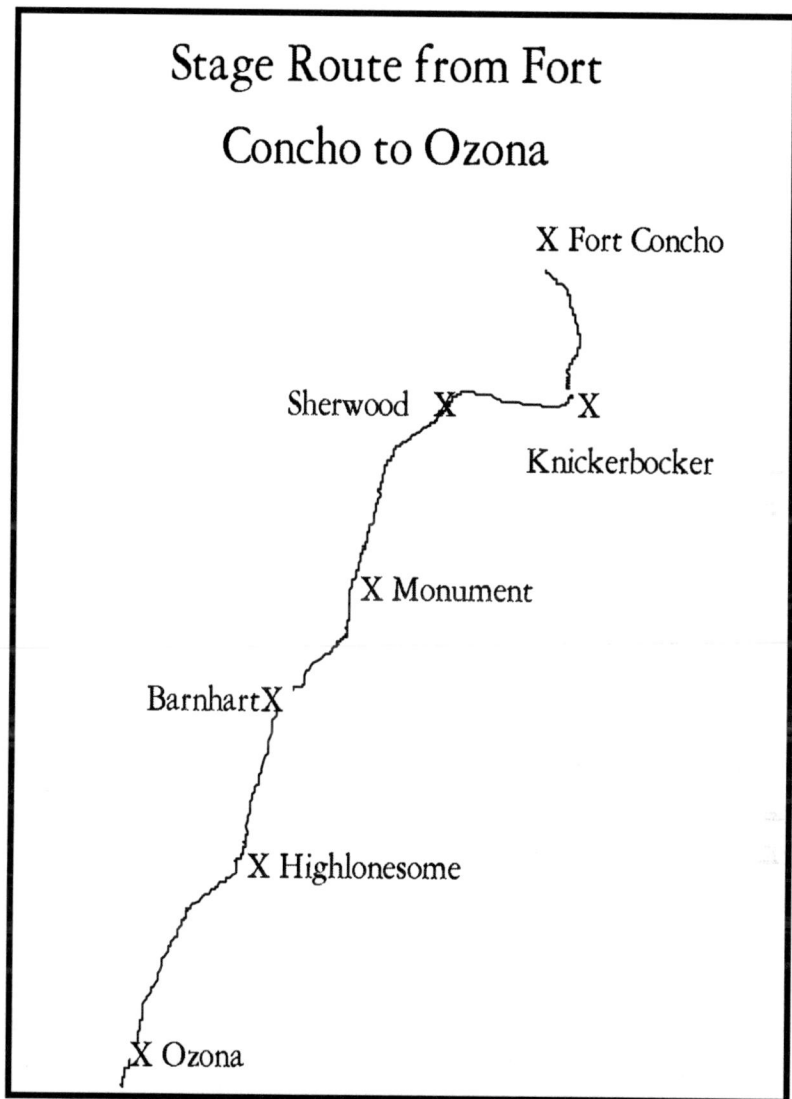

90 percent of their time repairing the harnesses for the stage lines.

Drivers of this 80-miles route from Fort Concho to Ozona used a team of two or four horses and made this long stretch by changing them four times: at Knickerbocker, Sherwood, Monument, and High Lonesome. These lengthy stretches passed through grassy prairies, rolling hills and some cactus covered deserts. Newton not only provided express service for the mail, but he also had daily passenger service between these two points. If a person wanted to catch the stage in Ozona so he could travel to San Angelo, he notified the company ahead of time.

Then the driver left the barns about four in the morning and circled around to pick the passenger up at his house. Breakfast was served much later at the first stage stand, High Lonesome. The next meal, dinner, appeared in Sherwood and the stage pulled into San Angelo about nine or ten that night. The stage driver encouraged his passengers to eat when they could because he stopped primarily to change horses.

Some people might think a stage roared down the rough roads at a terrific speed, but this was not so. Although high-spirited animals strained at the bit as they anxiously ran the first few yards of the trip, the drivers slowed them down after a half-mile. For most of the trip the horses gauged themselves at a rate of about five miles to the hour.

Passengers on the stage didn't have it easy. In *Settler's West* by Schmitt and Brown, a passenger declared after being bumped and jerked for many miles, "I know what hell is, I just had twenty-four days of it." But most travelers thought riding a stage was preferable to walking over the hot, dry Texas countryside by foot.

D. E. Cocreham owned a stage line in the San Angelo area that made its rounds between San Angelo, Vigo, Fort McKavett, Knickerbocker, Sherwood, Ozona, Water Valley and Sterling City. He hired C. H. Rau, a wheelwright, to make his carriages. According to James Elder, great grandson of Cocreham, the stage station was on Third Street in San Angelo. Cocreham also had a freight yard in San Angelo. Although the hacks and stages were well made, Cocreham remembered the horses that made these rounds most of all.

He changed his horses as many as five times a day if he was making a long drive. Many different colors came under harness as he described the teams as the duns, the browns, the blacks, the bays, the paints, the sorrels, the roans, and the grays. He considered the "Gray Allens" as the fastest of them all. These horses appeared dark iron gray with flecks of red in their coats. They stood sixteen hands high and weighed about 1,200 pounds apiece.

Most drivers started their teams at a moderate speed, but Cocreham said that the grays slowly increased their tempo until they were at a dead run when approaching the next stop.

Just as horses yearned for the next stop and the feed that they would receive, some stagecoach drivers knew which hotels served the best food, so they anxiously awaited a stop at mealtime almost as much as the horses did. When stages arrived at actual towns, the fare was a little better than that eaten in remote stage stops.

Cocreham did remember two particular inviting places to test his palate: the Brock Hotel in Sherwood and the Kilpatrick House in Ozona. Stage riders often came to Ozona when court was to be in session. One day the owner of the Kilpatrick House had trouble with his hired hand, a Black cook who wanted to leave. The hotel owner told his guests that if his cook threatened to leave that day, he was "going to give him a good thrashing: please don't think I am trying to raise a disturbance." (His guests were probably lawyers.)

Newton wasn't the only stage driver who carried dignitaries. Driver Cocreham remembered the names of several of his regular customers who rode with him: Mr. And Mrs. Newton of Mertzon who took their honeymoon trip with him, Fayette Tankersley, Claud Hudspeth, Jim Farr, John Findlater, and Dr. Boyd Cornick, known for his work with tuberculosis. He also had Mr. Henderson, H. G. Trotter, R. F. Tankersley, West Texas' first white citizen; C. L. Broome, M. O. Davis, Jose Tweedy who ranched at Knickerbocker, Col. W. L. Black, Judge Timmins, Judge Dubois, and other district court officials.

Stage drivers, the men who controlled their horses, were diversified people who held many jobs as they rolled the stage across the Texas plains. First requirement of their job was that they must know how to manipulate a team. They also had to be ready for an Indian or outlaw attack. The drivers had to be good shots with a rifle because not all stages had a rider next to the driver who could empty his rifle at the attackers.

Occasionally, accidents happened and the driver had to be in control if at all possible. Sometimes stages hit a mud hole, and it was the driver's responsibility to get the coach or hack pulled out. Broken wheels were another perplexing event. On top of these problems, some passengers were helpless little ladies or obnoxious, demanding men who required the driver's patience to be extended for long periods of time. Stage drivers had no easy job. If the average passenger knew what magic a driver performed with his reins, with a powerful brake, and sometimes a whip, they would

D. E. Cocreham owned a stage line that circulated through the small towns near San Angelo. Photo courtesy of his great-grandson, James T. Elder.

have appreciated more the person who sat in the driver's seat. Drivers with six horses had the pair nearest the coach, which were called the wheelers, harnessed to the rigid coach pole that controlled the turn of the front wheels.

The star route stage stopped at the Mary E. Lewis Hotel in Sherwood, 1905. Driver, W. E. Newton had the following passengers going to district court in Ozona: L. H. Brightman, San Angelo attorney; C. E. Dubois, San Angelo-Ozona attorney; Dan Brooks, district attorney; standing left to right; W. E. Newton in the drivers seat; and Judge J. W. Timmons, in back seat.

A swing pole, its purpose to hold up the doubletrees of the lead team, was attached by means of a stout hook to the end of the rigid pole. And the middle team (swing) team was harnessed to it with no slackness in the breast-straps or poles. The driver held these reins so he could have equal pressure on all six horses.

Once the driver left Fort Concho, he had four stops to make before he thundered into Ozona. Monument Switch, Texas, was ten miles southwest of Sherwood. It was named for nearby Monument Hill where a ranch house perched on its side and existed all alone except for the times the stage stopped. As the road left the bushy trees along Spring Creek, stage riders saw flat country with a lonely mesquite tree growing here and there. This prairie-like countryside continued until the stage reached the outskirts of Ozona, where craggy limestone hills covered the area.

Several horses usually poked their heads over the corral fence at Monument Switch, so the moment the bugle sounded from an approaching stage, a stagehand caught a fresh team and had them harnessed, ready to replace the tired ones covered with sweat and dirt. When the stagecoach left Sherwood traveling west, Monument was one of its first stops.

Location of this stage stop was on the Walter Noelke property. In 1977 he listed the objects found at the station ruins on January 7, and turned it into the Fort Concho Museum. The Kansas City Mexico & Orient Railroad came through that area in 1910. After this addition, ranchers established huge loading pens for cattle and sheep a few miles down the track at a place called Barnhart. By 1933 there was no stage stop, so the Monument location was called the Noelke Stop in honor of Walter Montgomery Noelke, an early settler of the area. During the first years of stagecoach runs, mail routes had a way of changing ownership in the blink of an eye. Watson and Kincaid had hardly begun their ownership of the San Angelo-to-Ozona line in 1905 before Jim Lackey underbid their contract. Suddenly they no longer owned the stage line.

Monument Stage Stop Remains

pieces of bone

tops and bottoms of snuff bottles

pieces of crockery

pieces of cinder

part of a white and flowered blue plate

necks and bottoms of purple bottles

pieces of glass, steel, and bricks

metal cans and many horeshoes

parts of a stove, a car horn, and a bike rim

belt buckle, square nails, parts of a spoon

Lackey was a busy man with ranching interests scattered from Sanderson to Barnhart, so he thought he would run stage horses while he ran his ranch. At the time of the stage purchase, he ranched around Barnhart, a burg that was a tent city at that time. His family lived where they could rather than where they preferred, so they became a part of the Barnhart Hotel clientele.

John Rochel saw the need for a hotel and café in Barnhart with so many ranchers and railroad workers milling about, so he built a large "L" shaped building with a tent for a roof. During the early 1900s, sixty men ate there daily, and Rochel partitioned the other section of his building into rooms. He had twenty-three families living there, including the Jim Lackey family. Jim's wife said, "In order for my family to eat in the café, we had to abide by Rochel's schedule. The Lackey family ate at 6 a.m." Running a stage took time away from Lackey's ranching, so he sold the stage line back to Watson in 1908.

The particular hack used in this area was built by the Jack Copeland Machine Shop in San Angelo. It could hold eight passengers and still have room for baggage and the mail. The stage usually carried 800 pounds on each run but could hold 1,200 pounds if necessary.

Certain stage drivers got a name for the way they handled the team. Frank Matchen drove the stage from Ozona to San Angelo and was known for his speed. His record was eight hours and 45 minutes for the distance labeled as 82 miles on today's map. He said, "I did it myself once or twice in nine hours." He added, "Usually we got in a hurry only when we had a passenger who wanted to catch a train. The railroad service came to San Angelo in 1888 but did not move west of the city until 1910.

Some people might think that stagecoach owners rolled in the money, but Ralph Watson painted a different picture. He said that he received about $1,800 a year for the mail contract at a time that his expenses totaled $7,200. These figures by themselves put Watson deeply in the red. The only way he could make a profit was by the income he received from express revenue and passengers.

People riding this route found no ornate coach awaiting them. Instead, they endured a bumpy, dusty ride in a four-wheeled hack with a white tarp top. Passengers perched on the two or three seats available. Their hack looked a lot like the next man's wagon except the tarp-like material stretched over a wooden frame could be lowered on either side of the hack to provide shade. Lack of wind made the travelers swelter in the heat when the tarps were lowered, so the ride was not too comfortable with shades up or down.

E. E. Foster remembered the mail coming in a southwest direction from San Angelo to Knickerbocker. He said, "As the stage rounded the point of the Knickerbocker hill coming from San Angelo, the driver would blow his horn." His notes of arrival quickened the pace of the stable boy who brought a fresh team from Jack Douglas' stables. From 1890 to 1913, Knickerbocker had its best years. This community included two saloons, a blacksmith shop, three stores, two hotels, and churches. The town got its start when Jose Tweedy brought sheep to graze along the nearby Dove Creek. He made his ranch headquarters about a mile north of the future location of Knickerbocker.

Jose Tweedy eventually developed a big mercantile store south of his home. The stage stopped at Tweedy's imposing wooden store, which housed everything from pickles in a barrel to horseshoes and harnesses. The stage passengers who entered this business ignored the enticing merchandise. Barrels of pickles, candy in jars, or canned peaches had no attraction for them. Instead, the dusty travelers made a bee-line for the water pail. Each traveler gulped a quick drink using the same gourd dipper hanging nearby. The gourd was passed from traveler to traveler.

While passengers got a drink, Delilah Johnson's helpers switched the team of fresh horses from her nearby corrals with the weary team. Moses Henry Johnson and Delilah left the south after the Civil War and came to San Angelo. Moses died suddenly, so Delilah moved to Knickerbocker where she operated the stage stop for several years. With fresh horses in the harness, the stage riders loaded up and headed westward toward Sherwood. On the way, they passed sheep and cattle grazing on the ranches. Cedar trees dotted the limestone hills as the passengers watched the landscape whiz by.

Jose Tweedy operated a mercantile store in Knickerbocker where the stages stopped either going to Fort Concho or Sherwood. Picture is courtesy of the West Texas Collection at Angelo State University.

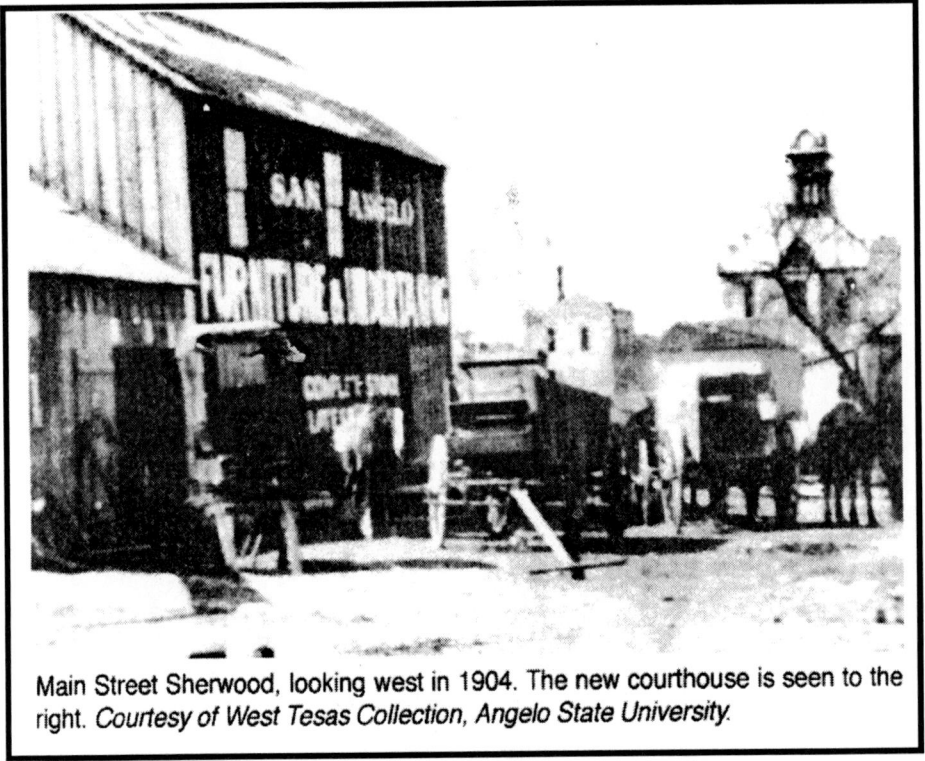

Main Street Sherwood, looking west in 1904. The new courthouse is seen to the right. *Courtesy of West Tesas Collection, Angelo State University.*

Chapter 4: Knickerbocker to Comstock

The first leg of this journey from San Angelo to Knickerbocker covered about 17 miles. As the refreshed travelers headed on toward Sherwood, their compass reading was set on due west. Leaving Knickerbocker, they crossed Dove Creek over the red bridge and traveled toward the setting sun as they bounced over low-lying hills. A few live oak and cedar trees dotted the hillsides.

Although this road is no longer visible, this dusty thoroughfare connected the two communities well into the 1940s. The first part of the road traveled over the present-day M. D. Bryant Ranch.

According to Jim Ridge who has lived on this ranch for a long time, a marker showing the county line was located on the Bryant Ranch and chiseled into the rock was "Tom Green and Irion." Although this stone is gone, it showed how the Sherwood-Knickerbocker stage crossed the county line from Tom Green's western boundary as it traveled to the eastern part of Irion County. This county line is about half way between the towns of Sherwood and Knickerbocker. Ridge also uncovered a stone marker that was about 100 yards west of the county line marker showing the mileage to San Angelo.

Upon examination of this slab, which is similar to a tombstone marker, you would think it was made by pouring cement in a rectangular form. The slab is about 2 and ½ feet tall and 15 inches wide. What makes this marker so unique is the fact that it sits in the middle of a large pasture many miles from any present-day road. If it was the stage route as believed, it angled west so that Ellis Draw paralleled it on the north side. The mileage marker is about five miles west of Knickerbocker.

The Jose Tweedy land lay next to the Bryant ranch, and a marker saying "20 mi to S. A." has been discovered on this ranch. As the stage continued its journey, it traveled thirteen miles among low hills dotted with green cedar bushes to leave Knickerbocker and reach Sherwood.

As the stage neared Sherwood, passengers could not see the town very well because it was nestled in a valley near Spring Creek. But as the stage neared this little burg, one driver named Crump always blew his trumpet. As the horses descended the outlying hills, the stage road finally dipped into

The marker that looks like a rock under the tree says, "S A 23 MI." Jim Ridge is standing to the right. Author's Collection. Courtesy of Jim Ridge and the M. D. Bryant Estate.

civilization and continued among occupied houses. Kids ran outside their homes to wave and yell at the driver. Nora Gentry remembered that as a child she saw the stage come in front of her house as it left Sherwood on its way to Ozona.

Stages often pulled into livery stables to change horses, and Sherwood had several such businesses. Bill Carr's stable had fine horses and buggies to rent. He had space for the stage horses so that a fresh team was always available. Bill's biggest customers were drummers, or traveling salesmen.

Bill met them as they left their stagecoach in Sherwood or at the train station, which came to San Angelo. Many drummers wanted Bill to drive the buggy and take them wherever they could sell their goods. One sales

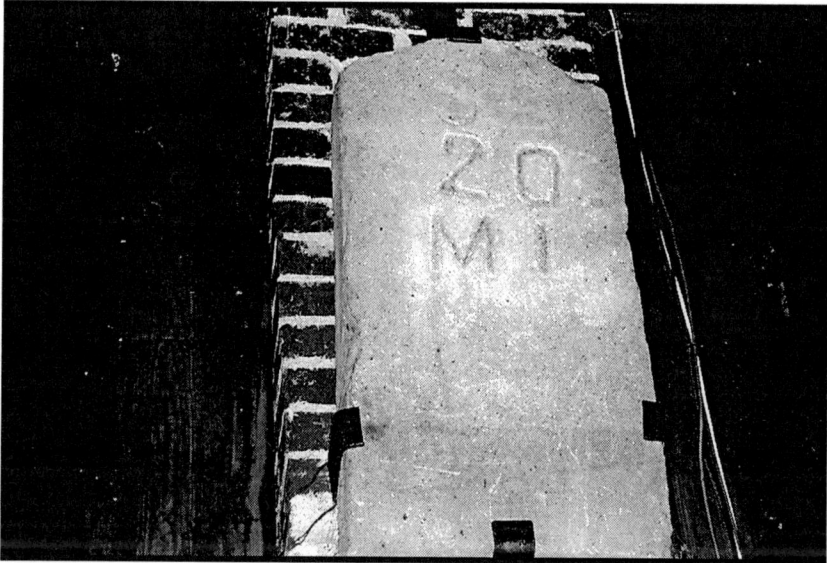

This marker says " 20 mi," and is displayed in the
Twin Mountain Steak House at the western edge of San Angelo, Texas.
Photo is Courtesy of the Twin Mountain Steak House.

person asked Bill to drive him to Ozona, which was about sixty miles southwest of town. Along the way, the salesman complained to Bill that he saw no houses. He wondered why his company sent him to this God-forsaken place. Bill laughed when he told the story because the salesman finally sold his specialty - windmills. Once he found the ranchers, he did a great deal of business.

When Bill Carr wasn't changing stage horses or escorting drummers around, he kept the local clients happy. He boarded horses owned by people in Sherwood, so he had to be sure they had their daily feed. Occasionally a young man rented one of his buggies so he could court his sweetheart.

If the stage horses weren't kept at Bill Carr's livery stable, they probably were at Moore's Livery Stable. W. P. Moore bought his stable in Sherwood March 17, 1893. While he worked with horses, his wife managed the nearby Brock Hotel. With such jobs, they kept the travelers as happy as they could with food and transportation. Cap.

Coffman was the handy blacksmith in Sherwood.. Although he often worked on stages, he could also repair hacks, surreys, or buggies.

After the stage passengers from Knickerbocker got to taste some food at the Brock Hotel, they were quickly ushered onto the stage. The next leg of the journey stretched before them, still 60 miles away from the next town, Ozona. They rode in a hack even if it was spruced up a little with a fringe around the top. If the weather had recently been dry, the stage driver probably used only two horses. Days of rain forced the drivers to use four horses because the creeks were harder to get through.

From Sherwood, the stage turned due south at the courthouse square. As they rounded this corner, they could see the two-storied rock jail that set in the southeast corner of the courthouse square. Prisoners were known to shout at people who passed by their window, but few could be heard over the noise of hoof beats on the limestone rocks. These passengers knew they would be driving over some low hills headed toward Ozona.

When the stage driver or freighters came down the south road into Sherwood, drivers applied the brakes to keep the horses and load from going too fast. According to W. A. Pringle who drove freight wagons in this area, when drivers got close to this hill, they chained the back wheels together so they scooted down the hill very slowly. Such loaded wagons and stages wore ruts in the limestone hill south of Sherwood.

When Mr. Pringle wasn't busy driving the stage, he was usually found driving a freight wagon. His main destinations were between Ozona and San Angelo. William Alexander Pringle received the title of "the 28th homesteader in Crockett County" when he resided in the town of Emerald.

Emerald, established in 1888 seven miles east of present-day Ozona, has an interesting history. A driller tapped water there at 540 feet below the surface. With this discovery, Railroad Commissioner T. A. Wilkinson encouraged the railroad company to help build this town. The company built windmills, put up tanks, a store and a schoolhouse, but all of this progress was short lived. Emerald lost its residents when Ozona became the county seat.

Emerald resident W. A. Pringle admitted to his grandchildren many years later that whiskey barrels often became his freight, and he had a secret way to open the barrels for a drink along the way. Each container was a 10-gallon oak barrel. He could stick a hot pin in the hole where the brand was placed on the barrel. After he had a little toddie, he could reseal the brand.

Men of different ages drove stagecoaches at this time. Lewis Smith of Rankin, only twelve-years old at the time, happened to be on hand when an emergency occurred on the stage line. Suddenly he became the substitute driver. When asked years later why someone so young drove the stage, Lewis said, "I drove the stage because there was nobody else."

As the stage pulled out of Sherwood, on its way to Ozona, the driver knew he had quite a trip to make. Several miles down the road heading south from Sherwood, the stage would be above the springs of the river, so it crossed a shallow Spring Creek and continued its southwestern route. The rest of the way to Monument, this trip bounced over solid rock roads interspersed with some dirt flats. After visiting Monument, the next stop was High Lonesome, and then the passengers would eventually see the sites of Ozona in Crockett County.

The High Lonesome stage stop was nine miles east of present-day Barnhart. According to Troy Williams, at this stage stop riders enjoyed some good drinking water. The hard part was getting to the water since it was 120 feet below the surface in a hole. The cave-like structure holding the spring was at the 09 Ranch Headquarters.

Troy said that one time a calf fell in the hole. Cowboys couldn't lift it out of the well at such a distance, so they put another plan in action. They butchered the calf while it was in the hole and hosted up pieces they could lift more easily. Hearsay indicates that the steaks cooked that day were pretty tasty.

The High Lonesome stage stop, built in 1902, served the last commercial stage line in Texas. Stage line employees usually kept ten horses in the corral ready for use. Although the countryside around High Lonesome was very flat, the stage had to cross Buckhorn Draw on the way to Ozona. Crossing this dry creek bed during dry times caused no problems, but this forty-two miles long draw filled with rushing water quickly when a rain came. At such time, stagecoach riders had to be careful.

The open spaces of West Texas began to put on a different appearance

Stage Route from Ozona to Comstock

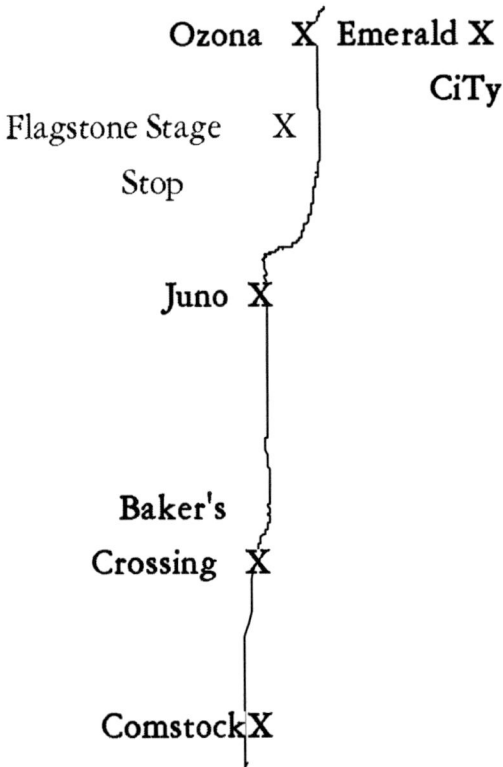

Ozona   X   Emerald X

CiTy

Flagstone Stage   X

Stop

Juno   X

Baker's

Crossing   X

Comstock X

Sketch by the Author

about the time that stagecoaches ran their last routes. After ranchers built wire fences around their property, it was harder for stage drivers to make very good time because they had to open too many gates. It was difficult even for Walter Dunlap who said there were thirty-two gates between Ozona and San Angelo at the time he was a stage driver.

W. A. Pringle and wife, Victoria. Pringle drove stagecoaches and freighted in the Sherwood – Ozona area. Courtesy of Wanda Lloyd, granddaughter of the Pringles.

Someone asked him how he kept his job with the stage for two years on that tough route. Walter replied, "I jumped off the stage while it was headed toward the gate, I opened it before the team got there, and then I ran to catch up with the horses after they cleared the gate. I had better times than any other drivers." It might have helped that he was small and wiry, too. Walter explained that the 83 miles from Ozona to San Angelo took 9 to 10 hours in ordinary weather, but during one rainy spell, he said he and the stage labored for 20 hours. The Ozona to San Angelo trip, like most stage journeys, had a relay station about every 20 miles.

In the Ozona area, a Mr. Hartley kept the dust stirring with stages that moved from town to town. In July of 1906, He partnered with Watson, but by January of 1908 the local paper mentioned Hartley and King as proprietors of the stage line.

By 1908, some of the stage hacks changed their appearance. Ralph Watson who drove the stages starting in 1902, decided to replace horses with Model F Buicks. They were spruced up with carbide lights, two-cylinder motors, and chain-driven side-winders. While the time for the trip from San Angelo to Ozona shortened from nine hours to six, the fare increased to $7.50 one way or $14 for the round trip.

Just before someone jumped to the conclusion that Watson was raking in the dough, they better listen to his expenses. "Tires were high and I did well to get 3,000 miles out of one," recalled Watson. "Gas was a dime a gallon." He admitted that he kept some horses for muddy weather and for the three-a-week express runs.

When the Orient railroad reached Barnhart in 1910, Watson could read the handwriting on the wall. Stage lines and freight wagons would quickly become a thing of the past, so he sold his teams of horses and hacks. He traded the Buicks to Jack McKee for a house and lot. At that time, the stagecoach driver went into the sheep business rather than teach school again.

Troy Williams once told a story about Sam Cox who often drove the stage to Ozona. He lived there, so the horses, as well as Sam had a rest when they hit town. He usually left the hack at the livery stable until the stage made its next leg of the journey. After making a run to Ozona one time, Sam left the stage and walked home. He rested awhile before he decided to play some baseball with a group of townspeople. After the game commenced with Sam as pitcher, he was very surprised to see several of the city fathers running toward him. Their distressed look triggered his memory.

At that time in 1905, the Ozona Bank had ordered $15,000 in cash to be delivered to them by way of the stage. Sam's last run was supposed to have the money on it. When the gentlemen asked Sam about the whereabouts of the cash, he apologetically told them he left it on the stage in a valise. That answer had the city fathers really worried, so they quickly raced to the livery stable. When they spied the valise at the exact spot where Sam left it, the bank owners quickly counted the money and breathed a sigh of relief. All the $15,000 rested safely in the bag where Sam left it.

In 1891, Ozona's streets filled with wool-loaded wagons as well as freighters carrying supplies for ranchers. By the fall of that same year, Ozona had a post office complete with postmaster, so there was a need for mail routes. A stage line carried the mail to San Angelo along with a brave soul or two who rode the hack as passengers. An additional route opened at that time, called a star route, to Comstock. A road connecting Ozona and Comstock was the first necessity, and a statement of its completion was dated February 25, 1893. The cost to build the road, listed as $500, was paid by the Comstock people providing $100 and the San Antonio merchants making up the balance. Store-owners wanted people of that area to come by train and shop in San Antonio.

By the early 1900s, the Southern Pacific Railroad ran through Comstock and the Santa Fe chugged its way toward San Angelo. Stage lines out of Ozona connected the town to the two railroad lines, one to the north and the other to the south. Frequent riders included preachers, teachers, drummers, young people going to school, and a few ranchers who used the train for long business trips.

Very few of the stagecoaches used in the run between San Angelo and Comstock were Concords. Instead the stagecoach companies owned hacks. Drivers had to do with one team of horses or mules unless mud required an additional pair. Although some people owned cars shortly after the year 1900, very few made their way to West Texas at that time.

Ozona had a busy stage schedule posted in 1906: the San Angelo Line left each morning at 6 a.m. while the returning stage arrived in Ozona at 6 p.m. that night. The stage left Ozona for Comstock at 5 p.m., and the returning stage came to Ozona at 8 p.m.

When passengers left Ozona on the Comstock run, they ate breakfast 20 miles down the road at a stand on the George Harrell Ranch. This location, called the Flagstone, was a stage station made of a large tent positioned over a floor of flagstones. Stage horses milled about in a rock pen and the stage stand included several tents as well as houses. This stop also had rock pens to hold pigs and cows.

A three-seated hack used on Crockett County stage lines in the 1890s. Notice "Ozona" printed on the canvas. Courtesy of the Crockett County Museum Society.

Wagon ruts are still visible here at a point 20 miles south of Ozona. According to V. I. Pierce, a local rancher, breakfast at this stop included eggs, bacon, and fresh-cooked biscuits. The next meal for the passengers was served at Juno. This little town included two hotels and about 45 families. Dinner could be pinto beans, meat, and canned corn or potatoes. On this route, people enjoyed supper at the Baker's Crossing. This family had a long table to serve everybody. After the final leg of the journey, passengers met the nine o'clock train at Comstock. Travelers were on their way to San Antonio.

George Karnes Deaton, born in October, 1855, lived part of his life in Central Texas. His father, Thomas Deaton, held the position of third sheriff hired in Comanche County. Lawmen had their hands full at this time with robbers and Indians in the area. The lawman's son, George, migrated to West Texas because of the stories he had heard about the ranching possibilities in that area. Deaton ran sheep first at Juno and then moved them to the Comstock area.

Deaton decided to delve into the stage business, so from 1888 to 1910, Deaton operated a six-horse stagecoach between Comstock and Ozona. On this trip the horses were changed four times. While running the stage business, Deaton also furnished freight wagons between the area towns. This endeavor required a lot of help, and Deaton had it. His sons, Oliver, John Henry, Arthur, Fred, and Clyde drove horse-drawn buggies, as well as wagons for their father. By 1882 people living in the Comstock area could hear the clang of railroad crews driving the rails into place. The Galveston, Harrisburg and San Antonio Railway connected the little town of Comstock with the rest of the world.

Ralph Watson drove the stages out of Ozona for several years. He also ranched in that area and raised a family. Courtesy of the Crockett County Museum.

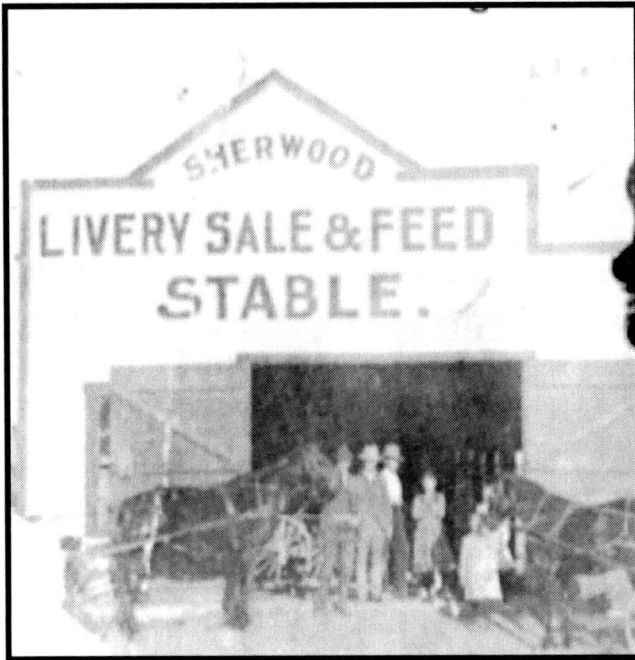

This livery stable was run by W. P. Moore in Sherwood. He bought the stable in 1893. Photo is courtesy of the Irion County Historical Society.

Chapter 5: San Angelo to San Antonio

The San Angelo to San Antonio stagecoach trip, about 200 miles, kept drivers and horses hopping because it was always busy. Stage riders who were lucky enough to stay overnight in San Antonio enjoyed the fifty-room Menger Hotel. William Menger built this inn out of rock quarried on nearby hills that are now called Breckenridge Park, a part of San Antonio. Stagecoaches leaving San Antonio bounced for many miles through cedar covered hills, which had streams gurgling at their base. The first stop was Leon Springs about 20 miles down the road in a northwesterly direction.

The next stops that riders enjoyed were Boerne, Comfort, and Fredericksburg. Some passengers looked forward to this last stop because they could eat at the Nimitz Hotel, owned by the father of E. A. Nimitz of San Angelo and Admiral Nimitz of World War II fame. This stage stop originally provided only six adobe rooms when built in 1855. However, its renovations between 1880 and 1890 changed it into

The Loyal Valley Inn, built by Philip Buchmeyer, remains abandoned but still standing as of 2004. Photo courtesy of Dan Gulino.

Fort Concho to
Fort Concho **San Antonio Stage**
Line

Lipan Springs

Kickapoo Springs

Menard

Ft. McKavett

San Saba River

Ft. Mason

Loyal Valley

Llano River

Fredericksburg

Comfort

Boerne

Leon Springs

San Antonio

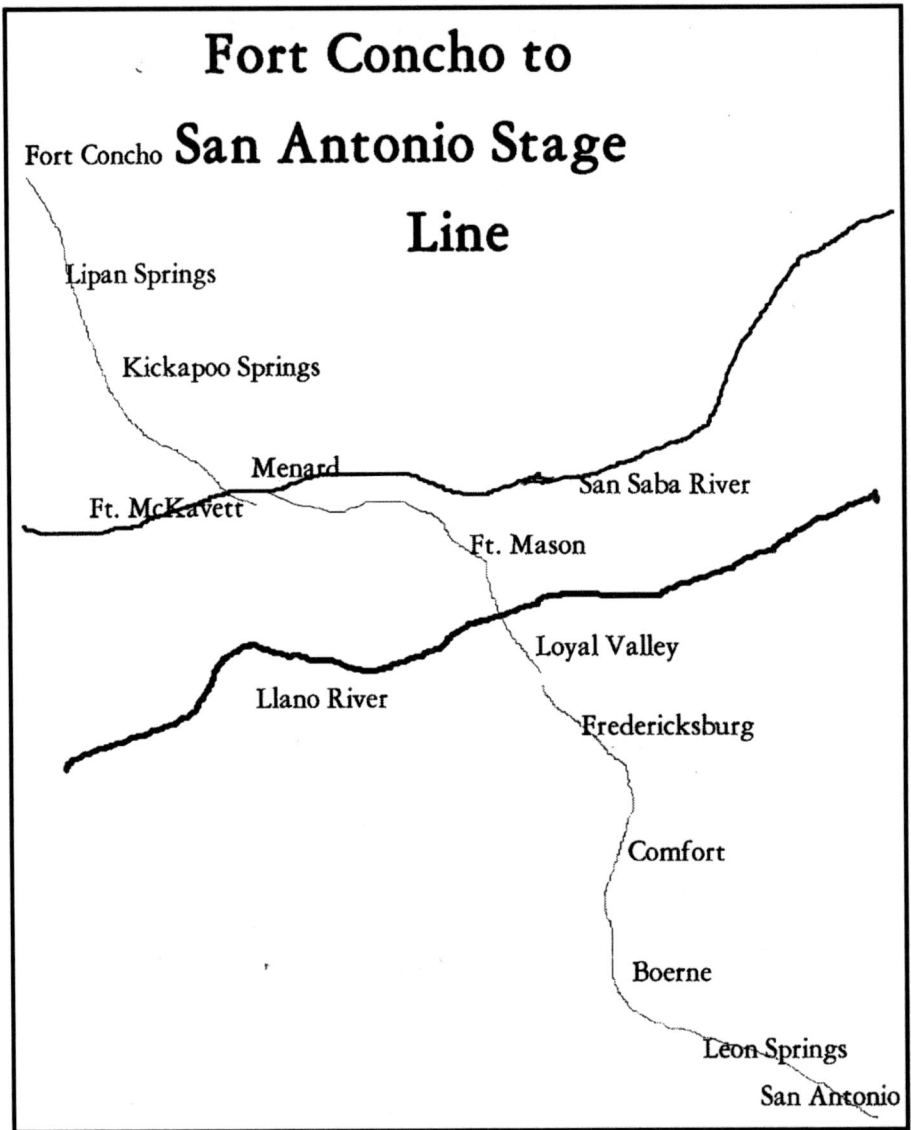

a "Mississippi Steamboat" shape with many rooms. The Nimitz name was also associated with an Inn in San Angelo. After leaving Fredericksburg, the stage drove to Loyal Valley, about 20 more miles in a northwesterly direction where Philip Buchmeyer built the Loyal Valley Inn in 1871. He made the building spacious with two-stories. This stage station was between Fredericksburg and Mason. Buchmeyer's stepsons Willie and Herman Lehmann were captured by the Indians several years before he built the stage station.

Little Willie escaped from the Indians in nine days and returned to a normal life, but Herman stayed with the Apaches, and later the Comanches, for eight years. As an Indian brave, he raided against the Texas Rangers and white settlers.

When Willie finally returned to his family, he had a hard time adjusting to his new life and relearning the German language, which they spoke. At this time his parents ran the hotel, so he often embarrassed them by appearing before the guests dressed in war paint, leggings, and a breechcloth.

Once the passengers boarded the stage, it left Loyal Valley and then crossed the Llano River to stop at the Keller Store. The passengers' next stops would be Fort Mason and Peg Leg Station as they angled their trail more westwardly before they made it to Menardville. The terrain began to change west of this point as passengers noticed flatter prairies with an occasional mesquite bush cropping up here and there. The final set of stops included Splittgerber, Fort McKavett, Kickapoo Springs, Lipan Springs and back to San Angelo.

Lipan Springs are presently on the Rocking Chair Ranch some 12 miles southeast of San Angelo on FM 1223. After 1873 or 1874 the stage detoured around Fort McKavett. A separate hack line took the mail and passengers from Menardville to Ft. McKavett. This change shortened the ride from San Angelo to San Antonio by 22 miles. About this time, stages ran from San Angelo to San Antonio three times a week and twice a week to El Paso. Later the schedule changed so that stages departed on their route daily except Sunday.

Those leaving San Angelo had one escort going to San Antonio and two riding the trail to El Paso, for robbers continued to hold up the stages. Once the bandits attacked a stage leaving San Angelo and headed to San Antonio. Everybody was robbed, including a Lieutenant Colonel and a Major from the Fort. One fine looking officer from New York bragged about what he would do if he was ever face to face with bandits holding up his stage. His time came one day.

The stage he was riding lurched to a sudden stop. When the young man looked out the window, he saw masked riders talking to the stage driver, but no help was in sight. The San Antonio stage was robbed again. The talkative New Yorker was robbed along with everybody. For a long time after that, the New York soldier heard the laughter of several officers when his name was mentioned.

According to the 1870 U. S. Census taken at Fort Concho and nearby Ben Ficklin, Texas, nine men were working with the stage company. They called many places "home," most of which were from the South or Midwest. The roster of drivers was as follows with their age and home state or country:

Name	Birth	Age
Drivers		
John Hoffmaster	Kentucky	40
James Harper	Ohio	26
Timothy Brown	New York	35
John Welch	Ohio	22
Christian Meisner	Prussia	28
John Bobo	Tennessee	30
James Miner	Missouri	30
Stage Watchman		
Samuel Anderson	Tennessee	35
Station keeper		
George Wallace	Ireland	30

Businesses like the San Angelo Burnet and Northwestern RR Stage Line continued to improve and make changes to help their passengers. In September of 1885, they happily announced that they had new hacks that would be running in first class order. To any passengers who had ridden the more comfortable Concord stages, the hacks looked to them like somebody's wagon. They had no sides except some flimsy curtains meant to keep the dust and sunshine out. The stage owners also posted schedules and ticket price lists in the local papers, so people would know the cost.

Even though few large towns existed in West Texas at that time, many people rode the stages from one small community to another. Some of the passengers were discharged soldiers from the various forts. These men were given transportation on the stage with the understanding that their pass would be redeemed in San Antonio. Visitors came to see families at the various forts, and many officers in the army preferred to travel by way of stage when they went from one outpost to another. Prospectors, some heading to points westward, helped to fill the stagecoaches.

San Angelo Burnet & Northwestern RR Stage Line, taken from the San Angelo Standard Times newspaper	
From San Angelo to Kickapoo	$2.50
From San Angelo to McKavett	$4.50
From San Angelo to Menardville	$6.00
From San Angelo to Mason	$8.00
From San Angelo to Llano	$ 9.50
From San Angelo to Burnet	$10.60
From San Angelo to Austin	$12.00

At a later date, all stages headed northwest from San Antonio were of the Concord type – luxury if you ever saw it because these were the top of the line vehicles. Such conveyances held as many as nine passengers inside and two on top with the driver. The elevated seats on the front and rear boots of the stage were not very comfortable, so only the stout hearted rode on these.

For some stage drivers, the Civil War changed their life drastically, and Adam Rankin Johnson was one such man. Before the war, he drove stages for the Butterfield Overland Mail and called Burnet, Texas, his home. But during a battle in Caldwell County Kentucky, Gen. Johnson was accidentally shot by his own men. This tragedy caused him to lose his sight in both eyes.

Johnson overcame the experience of being a blind prisoner in the Union prison at Fort Warren and returned to Texas after the war was over. He was in the stage business now in a different way. Johnson worked as a contractor for the Overland Mail. While employed this way, he founded the town of Marble Falls, worked to develop the waterpower of the Colorado River, and founded the Texas Mining Improvement Company. Thomas S. Miller, once served under Johnson's leadership on the battleground and knew him in his later years. Miller said, "...perhaps no man has led a more cheerful and happy life."

The trip from San Angelo to El Paso, the other part of the San Antonio-El Paso Trail, directed riders in a southwestern path. A smaller stage, called the "swell bodied hack," made the trip. Such a conveyance could squeeze six people inside the coach and put two more outside. Most passengers carried little luggage except a pair of blankets, an overcoat and a six-shooter.

The rear boot outside the stage could carry as many as four trunks as well as the mail. The boot was constructed of leather and had a leather apron. The front boot carried the driver and one or two passengers. Whereas the El Paso bound stage always used mules, going back to San Antonio, a passenger might notice mules or horses pulling the stage. On the road to Loyal Valley the driver demanded an extra team because of a bad hill on that route.

The stage stopped about every 20 miles, so the riders knew they could look forward to a drink of water at some stations and meals at others. New teams of horses or mules pranced nervously as attendants moved them from their pen to the waiting stage because they were ready to make tracks. Once connected to the traces, these horses were stomping nervously, ready to go. In San Angelo May 3, 1884, Mr. and Mrs. L. B. Harris, Mr. and Mrs. Childress and family, along with Mrs. Eugene Cartlege and son, and Walter Harris left for a pleasure trip to San Antonio.

This entourage included so many people that the stage company provided three hacks. These conveyances were a wagon with two or three seats that were protected overhead by a tarp-like material attached to the four corner poles to make a flat top. Hacks were not luxury items as the well-made Concord stages professed to be. The latter had wooden sides, enclosed with doors.

After a customer rode a few miles in the best coach made, they often complained of harsh conditions that they had to endure. Demas Barnes, an experienced rider, rode stagecoaches across America in the 1860s. He said they were usually overcrowded with three passengers squashed together in a tiny seat, one of them usually a woman holding a child. He described passengers in the seat facing you jammed against your legs while hat boxes and valises were ready to tumble from their perch above your head. Besides the noise of the harnessed horses galloping, babies cried inside the coach while the driver swore from his perch outside. The mood was not always harmonious, to say the least.

Passenger Demas Barnes said, "I never slept over at a stage stop because the dirty pallet provided as a bed and the unclean surroundings caused me to miss any sleep that might be forthcoming." He also feared losing his place on the stage if he stopped for the night and had to wait until another coach arrived with a seat available.

The weather usually showed passengers one extreme or another. If a person traveled in the summertime, the temperature inside of the coach might climb to 105 degrees or more. All passengers would share a fine black powder that covered their clothes and skin. At the other end of the weather picture, wintertime brought icy cold wind and snow, which silted through the windows much like the dust. If passengers tried to sleep at night, a sudden lurch of the coach might bring everybody out of their seat and into the floor. However, most passengers survived the trip in spite of the challenges.

Charles Bain owned some stage routes traveling in and out of San Antonio. On these trips, stage riders could use Bain coaches to travel from Boerne to Comfort on Sundays, Wednesdays, and Fridays. He also had a route traveling from San Antonio to Lavernia and Sutherland Springs on Mondays, Wednesdays, and Fridays.

If a passenger happened to stop in Boerne during the 1860s, he might be fortunate enough to spend the night at Ye Kendall Inn. Built in 1859, the building acted as a gathering place for many people such as lawmen, army officers, cattle drovers, and frontier celebrities.

Schedules of the stage lines changed from time to time to accommodate passengers, as well as the mail. For instance, on May 10, 1884, the stages from San Angelo to Burnet left on Monday and Thursday nights instead of every night as they had been scheduled to depart. The stage owner explained that the mail would still leave daily.

After the stage left San Angelo traveling south, it passed through the Bismark farms that raised vegetables for the town people. It continued bouncing over mesquite flats covered with grass and cacti until it finally descended into a valley. This green, restful area along the banks of the South Concho River was often planted in grain or hay for the stagecoach passengers to see.

One of the stages' stops would have been the P. H. (Paddy) Mires farm about three miles south of modern day Christoval. Paddy settled in this area in the 1870s and built a gristmill on the springs near his house to grind corn and wheat for himself, as well as his neighbors. A friend of his named Jack Miller helped him build the Mires house, a large rock, two-storied building that accommodated his family as well as stage passengers for the night. In its lifetime, this house served as church, hotel, and as a dance hall for the neighbors.

Since the San Angelo-Sonora stage road passed by the Mires home, the family decided to take in weary stage riders as well as freighters passing down the same road. The corral for the horses was away from the house and downstream a short distance.

Home of Paddy Mires near Christoval, which was used as a stage stop, hotel, and residence in its day. Photo is courtesy of Steven Van Court.

One day a man and his son spent the night at the Mires house. Early the next morning the father sent his son to hunt their horses so they could hitch their wagon. While he was gone, the boy ran into a party of Indians. They captured him and killed him in full view of the people in the house. This hideous act left the grieving father too far from home to make funeral arrangements, so the boy was buried in the Mires Cemetery nearby.

By 1900 a new road stretched southward from Christoval toward Eldorado, so drivers made a choice upon arriving at this community along the South Concho. Some coaches struck out for Fort McKavett in a southwesterly direction while others directed their horses due south toward Sonora. People living in Christoval at this time remember a stage-driving preacher named Rev. Atkinson who not only drove the stage but also owned the stage stop at Christoval for a time.

Since this town by the river had two stage routes passing through, demand for hotel rooms increased. By 1901 Christoval had many visitors who came to take the mineral baths provided and receive treatment for an illnesses known as tuberculosis. George Holland left his ranch work to delve into the hotel business. His son, Bob, related, "Dad ..built a hotel in Christoval in 1901 catering to 'lungers.'" The "downtown hotel" kept only healthy people, so the San Angelo-Sonora Stage hack stopped at their doors. By 1905 George Holland bought the downtown hotel, which was L-shaped and two stories high.

Business must have been good because he tore that structure down in 1914 and built a three-storied hotel. As the stage left Christoval heading toward Sonora, the passengers traveled through open country with few trees. Their first stop was at the Mark Fury Ranch where they provided fresh mounts for the stages from 1894 to 1909. Theodore Jackson Savell, (1872 –1954) owned and operated this part of the San Angelo-Sonora line. The Fury Ranch, on Hackberry Draw, heard the horn blow to signal the stage's arrival six mornings a week.

Men who worked at the Fury Stage Stop watered the horses at a nearby dirt tank and gave them feed. This stop supplied fresh horses for the two stages coming and going from Christoval each week. C. C. Doty had experienced the ups and downs of pioneer life before he signed on as a stage driver. When he first came to Christoval with several thousand sheep, he thought he would soon be rich. However, the drought, along with his management techniques brought about bankruptcy. Some people thought he drove around in his buggy too much rather than tending his sheep.

Doty was a determined man, so one failure did not stop him. Doty's next venture was that of postmaster at Christoval. When the authorities asked him to name the location, he wanted to call the place "Alice" after his girlfriend. The postal department refused that name, so he sent in "Christopher" in Spanish called "Christobal." They read it wrong and called the place "Christoval." A fire in the post office put Doty out of business again, so he took his turn driving the stage. He filled in as driver to make connections in Eldorado. What time C. C. Doty wasn't driving a stage, he was on the seat of a freight wagon. He said they were slower than coaches, because it took a wagon three and a half days to travel from Sonora to San Angelo, a trip that totaled about 65 miles. Doty knew he had to stop his wagon at different ranches to load or unload supplies, so he wasn't very speedy along the way.

Marker between Christoval and Eldorado showing the location of the Mark Fury Stage Station near Hackberry Draw. Author's Collection

Another leg of the journey from San Angelo to Eldorado passed through the J. D. Ernest Ranch. Mr. Earnest provided a change of horses at his stop also, which was called Hackberry. He related that muddy roads were hard on the stage horses, so when a big rain fell, the passengers had to jump out. They lent a hand and pushed the coach out of the mud holes, but what this did to their good clothes was best not mentioned.

When the coach was within five miles of present-day Eldorado, it came to a community called Verand, which was settled in 1890 with a stagecoach station, a store, post office and hotel. Fresh horses now pulled the coach onward toward Sonora, some twenty-five miles away.

Theodore Savell, along with his father and brothers, moved to Sutton County, near Sonora, in 1891. From this area, they operated a freight and stage line to San Angelo. Their service for people was not the speedy kind, explained Savell. He said, "The round trip to San Angelo by hack required six or seven days." Savell admitted that most of the freight was ranch supplies, so the passengers had to sit on top of the merchandise as they rode the Savell wagon from one ranch to another. This travel wasn't very speedy or comfortable.

William Farris settled in Irion County in 1910. While he managed a livery stable in Sherwood, he had a chance for an extra job as a stage driver. Luckily for him, Farris was hired to drive the mail route between San Angelo and Sonora. In his spare time, Farris drove around Irion County, and he noticed the railroad gangs driving the spikes to hold the rails in place from San Angelo to Mertzon. The railroad crew needed materials that fit in his wagon, so he changed jobs and became a freighter for the Santa Fe Railroad Company.

In the early years of stagecoaches, Indians and outlaws made life miserable for the passengers. After many people sent letters to army offices begging for help, their requests reached the government in Washington. Forts sprang up to protect the stagecoaches. In West Texas, the most notable were Fort Mason, Fort McKavett, Fort Concho, Fort Stockton, and Fort Davis.

Another problem that irked passengers was the fact they often couldn't find a stage line that carried them to the smaller towns. Short stage lines soon developed like the one between Kerrville and Mountain Home, so that travelers could connect to large stage lines.

Adolph Oehler bought a farm near Mountain Home, Texas in 1908. This location was about 20 miles northwest of present-day Kerrville. His son Herbert told of a stage stopping near their place for a change of horses. The hack that Roy Kemp drove had three seats with an oilcloth-covered top. The curtains were also of oilcloth, and they had isinglass windows. Most of the time, the curtains were rolled up so the passengers could view the countryside, but when it rained, the driver had to be sure the curtains were rolled down and fastened. Kemp operated a stage line through Mountain Home that included Kerrville as one of his destinations.

The Oehlers decided to provide a pen for the stage horses and a pasture for them to graze when they weren't working. They hired a person to work at the stage stop, so they had to provide housing for him. The worker they employed, lived in a tent under a big walnut tree at the creek.

The hired hand unharnessed one team and hitched the fresh one when the stage made this stop. He also kept the horses fed, watered, and shod. Men such as Mr. Rainey and Mr. McMickle had the job of stagehand, but Oehler's sister-in-law, Emma Heimann, also cared for the horses for a period of time. From Mountain Home to Kerrville, the stage driver usually had a four-horse hitch. But the pull between Mountain Home and Junction was tricky, especially in the mud. Sometimes this route needed six horses. Heavy freight wagons full of wool and mohair often made the trip between Junction and Kerrville. These wagons had the tendency to make deep ruts in the ground if it had rained recently.

River crossings were another problem, especially after a rain. The road between Mountain Home and Kerrville crossed Johnson Creek twelve times. When the hacks were late, men like Mr. Rainey lost their patience. If he couldn't hear the stage coming, sometimes he would walk up and down in front of the Oehler's house, where the stage stopped. He would chant to the horses, "Come on, Baldy, come on, Baldy." He knew that Baldy should be coming down the road from Kerrville any minute.

If the weather was cold, the Oehlers invited the passengers to come inside their house and warm themselves. Son Herbert remembered some guests who brought bricks into the house to warm. Then they wrapped the brick in a tow sack or piece of blanket so it would retain its warmth for the next leg of the journey.

Herbert also mentioned his family's outhouse as being available for the passengers. He said the structure was a two-seater and provided either corncobs or the Sears Roebuck catalog for their use. Surely the passengers appreciated these conveniences, which were provided for them at that time.

Robbers often appeared in unexpected places. Solomon Maxwell's ferry was one such example. He ran the first ferry near Bluffton on the sometimes very deep

Colorado River. He cut the gunnels of cottonwood trees on the Little Llano River, and purchased the flooring in Austin. After Maxwell built the ferry, three strong men

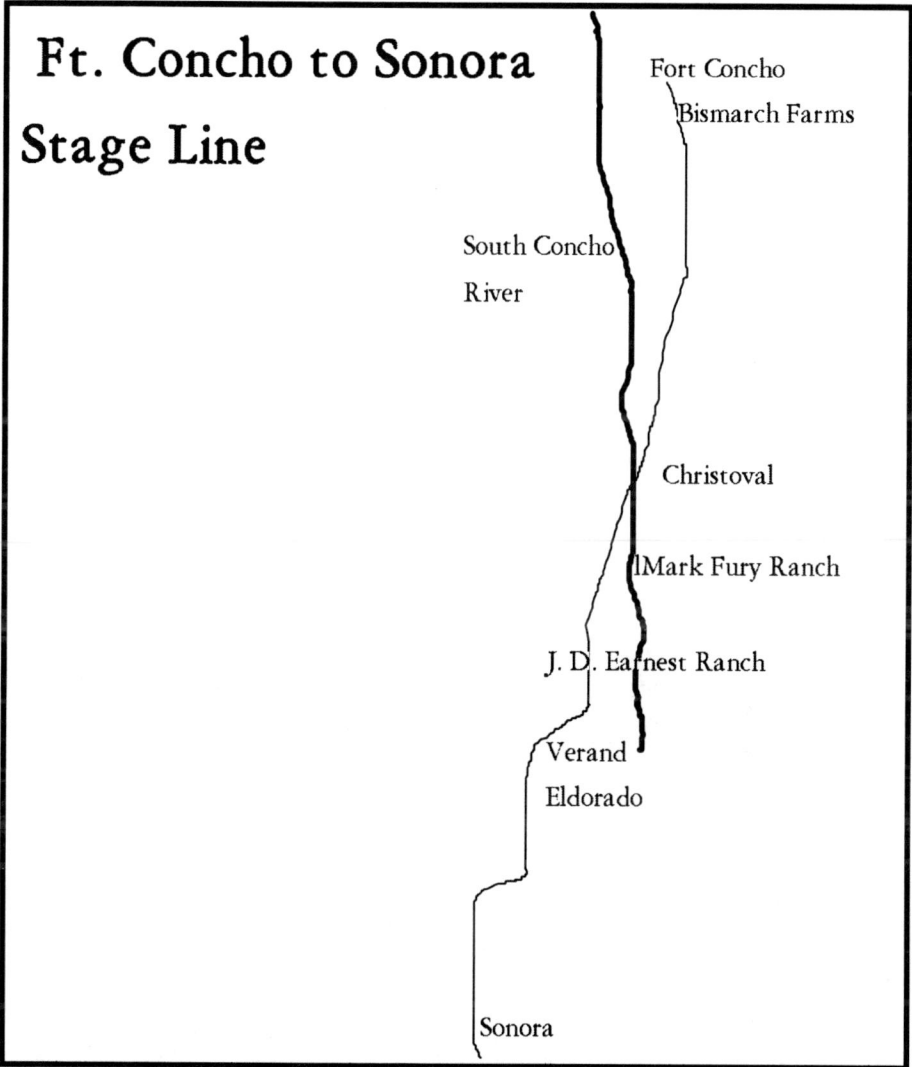

Ft. Concho to Sonora
Stage Line

Fort Concho

Bismarch Farms

South Concho
River

Christoval

Mark Fury Ranch

J. D. Earnest Ranch

Verand
Eldorado

Sonora

pulled this 30-feet long boat across the river. The freighters depended on this crossing, because all wagons going east or west passed over this ferry. Bluffton also connected stage lines moving from Austin to Mason and Fort McKavett.

One day Maxwell's ferry unknowingly carried two armed outlaws who rode onto the ferry horseback. Also loaded on the same ferry was a load of fat pigs. Something scared the pigs, they bunched up on one end, and the ferry promptly sank. The outlaws swam out of the river and disappeared before people realized who they were.

This ferry was active for twenty-five years, and old timers remember dancers twirling their partners on the ferry at special get-togethers. Charges for use of the ferry were as follows: 50 cents- single team; 75 cents- double team; and 25 cents – horseback riders. The stage stand was located at the corrals near a Bluffton hotel, so the stage line could make its necessary stops and passengers had lodging for the night.

For the time-period of the 1800s, stage lines that ran on schedule and stopped at good hotels were much in demand.

Stage at Bluffton, 1890, waiting to cross the Colorado River by ferry. Elder Black, Methodist presiding elder, is shown at left of the stagecoach. Courtesy of Llano Gem of the Hill Country, by Wilburn Oatman.

Chapter 6: From San Angelo to Abilene

Early Texas settlers needed a road westward from Fort Worth, and the military solved that problem. In 1851 troops built a road from Fort Worth to Fort Belknap, which happened to cross over Cement Mountain. Years later troops from frontier forts and stage lines continued to travel this route. The Fort Worth-El Paso Mail passed through this area until 1876.

A special event in Fort Worth, Cow Town, affected stagecoach service in many small towns in southwestern Texas. On July 19, 1876, Fort Worth established a railroad station that linked Texans to many towns. Now a stagecoach line left Fort Worth as it traveled southwestward through Granbury, Stephenville, Dublin, Comanche, Brownwood, and Coleman on its way to Fort Concho. Charles Bain and Company owned this line. A year later, the railroad lines reached San Antonio. Mr. Bain jumped on this new addition and advertised that he would connect passengers to San Antonio just as he had with Fort Worth.

By 1880, Charles Bain had his business operating out of San Angelo. In that year, the U. S. Census stated that Bain, a 47-year old contractor, was single but had seven unmarried white men listed in his household. These individuals proved to be people who worked for him on the stage line.

Name	Age	Birth-place	Occupation	Father's home
Charles Bain	47	Mo	Contractor	Scotland
Elijah Bates	52	TN	Laborer	PA
J.B. Taylor	19	AL	clerk	GA
B.D. Bennett	22	TX	Laborer	AL
Harry Turner	28	Eng.	Laborer	England
George Whitman	31	AR	Laborer	AR
George Scott	27	MO	Laborer	OH
Edward Biford	17	TX	Blacksmith	VA

Charles Bain's stages, that had Fort Worth as their destination, left San Angelo traveling east and had their first stage stop at the small community of Van Court. William C. and Ida Dicky set up a stage station about one and a half miles east of the present town of Van Court. W. S. Kelly organized this route for the El Paso Mail Company that stopped at the Dicky's place. Although Ida and William Dicky lived there, Kelly himself applied for the first post office in that area. He named it "Van Court" after his new bride, Mary Ann Van Court. W. S. Kelly kept his finger in many businesses around San Angelo, such as buying buffalo hides and running a mercantile. Directing the stage and running the post office at Van Court gave him a few more titles to add to his name.

Such stages as those stopping at Van Court could have Fort Griffin as one of their final destinations. This journey, as the crow flies, would be about 118 miles on a northeasterly direction, but the stage weaved from one little community to another until it finally reached Albany and then Fort Griffin. The miles stretched out a bit more than the crow flew.

Although Fort Griffin had a business recession in the late 1870s, C. Bain and Company started a stagecoach circuit there in 1877 that made Fort Griffin the town as its center. This route stretched from Weatherford to Jacksboro, Fort Belknap and then to Griffin. Bain's high expectations were obvious by the fact that he bought two new coaches from Concord, New Hampshire for this route.

Passengers leaving San Angelo or Fort Griffin now had a variety of destinations from which to choose. From 1879 to 1882, James Hammell owned a contract for the route #31591, which connected Fort Griffin to Fort Concho. The return trip on this line passed through Chimney, Phantom Hill, Buffalo Gap, and Fort Chadbourne.

On the road between Ballinger and Abilene, there also existed several stage stops. About sixteen miles east of Winters, a stage stop called Blue Gap was established February 14, 1878, where there was a gap in the mountains. Inhabitants of this one-room log cabin greeted stage passengers who rode along the winding cow trail misnamed as a road. In the next eight years, men who served as postmaster at Blue Gap included James K Paulk, B. F. Sullivan, J. J. Craig, and Alfred Hanscomb.

A stage stop that was called the half-way point between Ballinger and Abilene was situated about five miles northeast of present-day Winters. Bill Gee ran this stage stop, which was near Antelope Creek, but his main water supply was a strong well built on his place. Residents of this area remember seeing a hack with white canvas top and curtained sides pull up to Bill's stop. While passengers stretched their legs, fresh horses trotted from the nearby pens.

Blackwell, another stage stop in this region, had stages running through its town as late as 1907. This community was about halfway between Abilene and Fort Concho, which made it fifty miles from either. People in this town saw the mail leave by way of stage from their community and head toward Olga, a town about four miles from Blackwell. The Orient Townsite Company originated the burg called Blackwell, which had busy streets filled with shoppers in the early days. The Orient Railway made its way through town in 1908, but stages still did their part to deliver people as well as the mail to the smaller communities in the region.

Fort Chadbourne was less than 10 miles east of Blackwell, and the mail there continued to be delivered long after the fort was vacated. According to *The Texas Gazeteer*, this burg of twenty-five people still had a semi-weekly stage coming from Buffalo Gap in 1884. The postmaster, H. H. Luckett kept the mail going while J. B. McCutchen, a local rancher, manned the general store.

In the early 1900s, people in Fort Chadbourne heard that the Mexico and Orient Railway was headed their way. Citizens scrambled to move their houses several miles west to enjoy rail service. The train eventually took the place of the stage, so in 1913 Allen LaFayette Cadile bought a hotel in Fort Chadbourne. He and his wife Ella took care of guests who rode the train. Allen also had a livery stable so he could drive travelers about the county once they left the train.

Another 1879 stage owner was Frank Conrad. His advertisements indicated that he also had stages to and from Albany, Graham, Fort Concho, Fort Elliott, and Mount Blanco. These communities north of Abilene included Graham, which was 58 miles northeast of Albany, and Fort Elliott, which was near Mobeetie in the Texas Panhandle. George Soule had ownership of the mail hack, which left Griffin on the way to Fort Concho.

Stage Lines North & East of Fort Concho

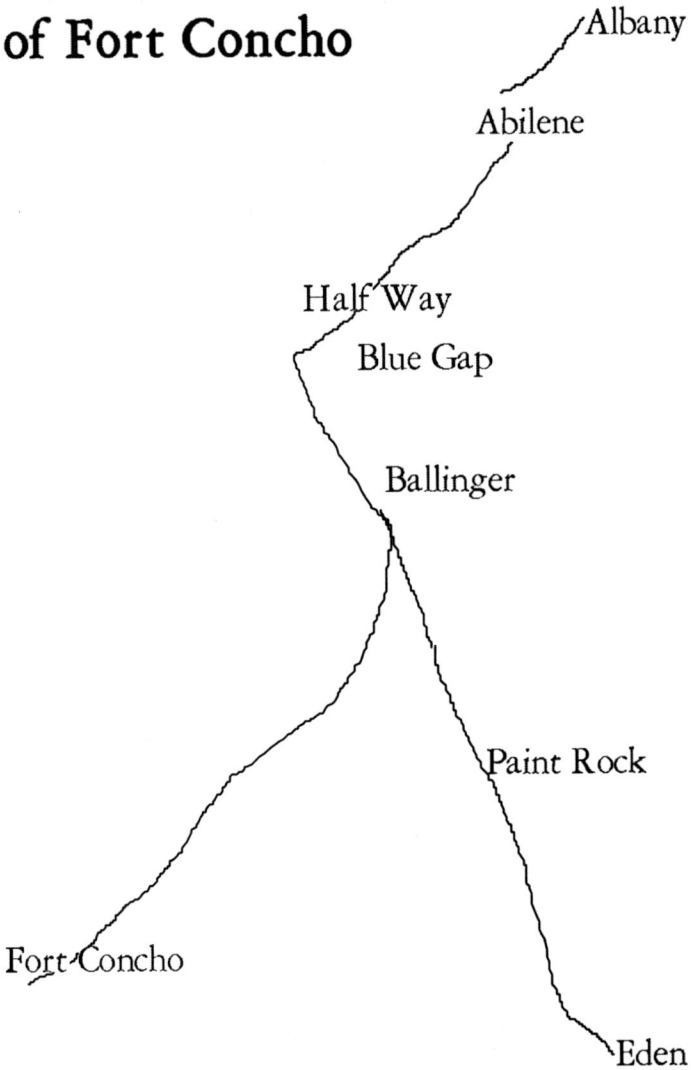

Albany

Abilene

Half Way

Blue Gap

Ballinger

Paint Rock

Fort Concho

Eden

Although the flag over Fort Griffin was lowered for the last time on May 31, 1881, its citizens thought their town could exist without the military because buffalo hunters and cowboys would keep business jumping. Fort Griffin had three saloons, four hotels or boarding houses, and one grocery store at this time. Two livery stables took care of the many horses.

A short route out of San Angelo that was owned by Bain connected Fort Concho with the Williams Ranch area in San Saba County. This route passed through Paint Rock.

While traveling through the ranch land between San Angelo and Paint Rock, the stage made at least one stop. About half way between the two towns, the stage slowed down at a very large barn owned by the ranching partnership of Loomis and Ostrander. Englishmen John Loomis and his partner Ostrander settled in that area in 1886 on 76,000 acres. Loomis built a rock house accompanied by a very large three-storied rock barn. When in use the top floor of the barn had rooms for the cowboys, and the below ground-level area was used by the servants. The ground floor was so large that a stagecoach could turn around in it. This part of the barn was later used as a fort.

Star route mail service was contracted to the lowest bidder and many individuals drove a hack or stage to deliver mail as well as passengers to small towns near Fort Concho. Communities that had a star route in the early years were Arden, Robert Lee, Sterling City, Sonora, Eola, and Eden.

Three-floored barn owned by Loomis and Ostrander Ranching Company. Courtesy of the West Texas Collection, Angelo State University.

In the 1870s, any stage coming toward Fort Concho crossed Indian territories and had to be prepared for an attack. White Horse was a renegade Indian who ambushed a stagecoach near Margaret Mountain September 30, 1870. This skirmish took place in southeastern Coke County near the present community of Tennyson, between Bronte and San Angelo. U. S. trooper Martin Warmser, serving as an escort, fought the Indians but was killed. White Horse continued to terrorize West Texas when he joined forces with Big Bow and attacked a wagon train in Crockett County April 20, 1872.

J. R. Barnett, owner of the San Angelo Stage, said he was changing the route from Paint Rock and the Colorado River stand so that as of July 1, 1884, he would run a daily mail hack. He felt this new schedule would improve connections with Coleman and Abilene.

At this time there were no stages to Coleman from San Angelo, but two years later, Captain Norton of Coleman visited San Angelo and spoke to people about the possibility of such a stage line. He soon put wings to his dreams because a hack owned by Norton and Roe left Abilene a few days later to travel through Runnels and Coleman. This particular stage line changed its schedule May 22, 1886, so that it left San Angelo at 7 a.m. standard time, which was 6:15 a.m. sun time instead of the previous 4 a.m. start.

Stages usually traveled at a pretty good clip as they moved through a town like Coleman, but drivers had to watch in this town for a riderless horse running down main street. Fred Sackett owned such a horse. This gentleman, born in Camp Colorado May 14, 1889, was very familiar with the town of Coleman. The local gossip had it that Fred would ride straight to the saloon when he came to town. He jumped off his horse and ran inside. His faithful saddle horse always galloped to the livery stable where he stayed until Sackett finished his drinking. When his horse came running through the streets of Coleman, people would say, "Fred's horse is coming, better get out of the way." Stagecoaches had to beware of this horse also.

In the 1870s, a community developed in the southwestern part of Coleman County called Flat Top. Richard Coffey built his ranch headquarters at this location in 1862. Because there was such a threat from the Indians, Coffey built several cabins for his cowboys and encircled them with a picket fence. One building that he made was a flat-roofed building that gave the place its name – Flat Top.

Coffey's headquarters was on a road that had a telegraph line stretched from Fort Concho to Fort Belknap. Since both military establishments were nearby, ranchers of this area had a ready market for their cattle. They sold beef to the forts. Flat Top also became known as a stage stand on the Fort Concho – Brownwood Line. About this time men built rock corrals at this place to hold the stage horses. The corrals probably provided better protection from the Indians than the picket cabins where the cowboys and travelers stayed. Large spaces between the picket timbers allowed too many arrows or bullets to fly indoors. The Flat Top post office stayed in existence from 1879 until 1881.

As interest in the Flat Top area diminished, more people migrated about 30 miles northwest to the new community of Ballinger. N. F. Bonsall operated the stage line between San Angelo and Ballinger at one time, but on June 29, 1886, he had other enterprises in mind. The Atchison, Topeka, and Santa Fe line made its way to this new community, and they wanted people to live there. The day that the train company sold Ballinger lots, people congregated in large numbers as the bidding went at a fierce pace. Bonsall worked as first engineer on the train that stopped in town that day.

Some shorter stage lines connected small towns and missed the larger burgs completely. The Ballinger to Menardville Stage Line, which was owned by H. D. Pear, connected Ballinger, Paint Rock And Eden to Menardville in 1890. This trip, starting in Ballinger, was a straight shot nearly due south to Menardville.

By the time the Menardville Stage Line was in business, Ballinger had the train puffing through its town, so many passengers needed a ride. The stage line was busy as it connected travelers to other towns after they got off the train.

In a different direction, a stage stop on the Wylie Ranch was located fifteen miles northwest of Ballinger. Since R. K. Wylie was one of the first settlers in Runnels County, he had to fortify his headquarters with a fort to protect his workers from Indian raids. Travelers visited his fort.

Another stage stop near Ballinger was located four miles southeast of town at a crossing of the Colorado River. A settlement by the name of Walthall grew up on the east bank of this river crossing where some citizens lived in dugouts.

From Ballinger the stage drove near the Painted Rocks on the Concho River. One mile west of Paint Rock some 1,500 pictographs were painted on limestone cliffs that towered 70 feet above the riverbank. Pictures of many shapes including birds, buffalo, and warriors still remain today visible in hues of red, black, yellow or white. These drawings gave the town its name.

Layered rock like this picture parallels the Concho River. Comanche Indians drew about 1,500 markings on these limestone ledges. Author's collection.

By 1884, Paint Rock had quite a few ranchers, so it was a shipping center for wool, hides, pecans and mutton. Freighters and trail bosses kept the economy going. In the early years of this town's growth, it had Methodist, Baptist and Presbyterian congregations, but they all met in the same building. At a later time they built individual church buildings.

Eden, 37 miles south of Ballinger, was one of those towns without a railroad so they depended on the stage for transportation. When passengers stepped out of the stage at Eden, they saw a post office and a school building as well as a general store, saloon and a jeweler. Eden's population in 1890 was about a hundred souls. Travelers often rode the stage onward to Menardville.

Passengers who rode to or from Menardville in 1890 noticed that it was a buzzing town with more than 150 residents. Their two-story courthouse was nearly twenty years old by this time as it watched over a church, a school, and several stores. Most families sold livestock, wool or hides to eke out a living there along the San Saba River.

Some stagecoaches moved between Menard, Eden, and Ballinger regularly. If a stage rider aimed for Ballinger as a night stop, travelers there were encouraged to stay at the Pearce Hotel for $1.00 a day. At this location, they could catch the stage every morning at 7 a.m. unless it was Sunday. From Ballinger a passenger could travel to Paint Rock for $1.50, to Eden for $3.50 and to Menardville for $5.00. Round trips from Ballinger to Paint Rock were $2.50, to Eden $6.00 and to Menardville $9.00.

Mr. Pearce not only had a hotel but he also handled freight and express on his stages. His advertisement mentioned his express office in Paint Rock, which was operated by E. M. Boykin. From this office a traveler could obtain hacks as well as horses.

If a person wanted to ship a package using the stage, they would have to pay a minimum cost of 25 cents. If a package weighed 100 pounds, it would take $1.50 to ship it from Ballinger to Menardville, $1.00 to Eden and 50 cents to Paint Rock.

By 1890, people in the Coleman area had a new way to travel from town to town; the train rails made it to their city. The Howell Livery Stable provided a buck board service for passengers to and from the Santa Fe Railroad Station in Coleman. In 1911, William Robert Hinds and his wife ran a boarding house and livery stable. Robert met the trains with his hack, and drummers hired him to show them the southern part of Coleman County. If the salesman was lucky, he met ranchers or farmers who bought his product.

Around 1890 to 1892, coal was discovered along the Colorado River near Rockwood. This town, in southern Coleman County about halfway between Santa Anna and Brady, was the area where settlers first named their town "Camp Creek" for the little nearby stream, but in the early 1880s, they changed the name to Rockwood. With the discovery of the black rock called coal, a boom hit the little community. Men came to dig in the mines while others brought their wagons hoping to take a load of coal to a nearby city and sell it.

DeWitt Ayers, born January 19, 1919 in the Rockwood community said the mines continued to be worked when he was a kid. He watched the little carts go into the open shafts empty and later saw teams of horses pulling the loaded carts outside. DeWitt also remembered the abandoned mines scattered over the countryside. The mining companies could no longer extract enough coal to make their work pay, so they left the shafts as they were.

But the sound of picks and shovels continued to ring in the abandoned mines because people needed fuel. DeWitt saw townspeople dig in the shafts so they could get enough coal to burn in their stoves. A high-phosphorus content made the mines a scary place to be. He said, "As a kid I saw smoke coming from some of the abandoned holes. My folks didn't want me playing around the mines."

When coal was discovered in Coleman County, freighters realized they had another product to ship. L. E. Page worked in the coalmines in the Waldrip community. When he dug coal in the mine, he received 50 cents a day, but he made $2.00 for every wagonload he freighted to nearby Brownwood. Patrick Hester also took his wagon to the coalmines. In 1903, he carried coal from the mines in Rockwood to Ballinger and to San Angelo.

A community called Bobo had a stage stand and as of 1886 a hotel was available for the riders. This location was near a crossing on the Colorado River, which was plagued with many problems. September 4, 1886, Corp Spellman drowned as the stage tried to cross the Colorado River. The stage horses drowned in the same accident.

J. R. Barnett introduced a mail route from San Angelo eastward that included Paint Rock in June of 1884. In September of that same year, the stage from Abilene was late making connections in San Angelo. The driver complained of bad roads and rain hampering his progress. In the spring of the following year, the owner posted a new schedule for this stage line. If a person caught the stage in San Angelo at 3 p.m., they would arrive in Abilene at 7 a.m. the next morning.

Lawmen were thankful that most of the men in this area believed in working for their money rather than stealing it. N. W. Deans was a good example. He came to the Ballinger area in 1878 to get a start in farming. He, like most young men, looked for a way to get a few acres, and he found a solution. He bought 320 acres, which was his for paying the back taxes owed to the state. Even though this arrangement was good, he needed money. Deans soon obtained a job as stage driver from Fort Chadbourne to Concho, a small community near Paint Rock.

Deans also made the run from Camp Colorado to Concho. This fort was in the northern part of Coleman County. Deans' son, Ed Dean, said about his Dad, "He had some skirmishes with the Indians while operating it." Although Fort Chadbourne had been in existence for many years, Indians still roamed the area. Deans, attacked by some of the Indians, was able to keep the stage going without too much bloodshed.

Deans had a wife to care for too, so he wanted them to have a good home. He began building on his rock house as he had time, but during the winter of 1880, his house still had no roof. A wagon sheet, stretched between the walls, kept the snow from falling on their bed. Babies did not wait for roofs to be finished, so on February 3, 1880, baby Ed Deans was born inside the rock house with a temporary roof.

Two years later, the Deans moved to Runnels City, the largest town around before Ballinger came into being. They bought an acre of land for 45 cents and decided on a new line of work. Deans and partners, Jim Holliday and Sterling Hathaway, ran a freight line to Abilene. Now they could load a variety of merchandise on their wagons to take from one town to another.

Stagecoach passengers could not stop the horses at nightfall as freighters did, so they spent many hours riding through the darkness of night. To accommodate them, stage owner Barnett decided to change his times. One June 20, 1885, he announced in the newspaper that the stage would now leave San Angelo at 3 a.m. sun time or at 3:40 Standard Time as it made its way to Abilene. He said, "Passengers can now make a trip in daylight arriving in Abilene at 7 p.m." In the same issue of the newspaper, a writer made fun of people who complained about the expense of keeping a horse in the livery stable. He said, "To save livery stable bills, buy a bicycle."

One morning in June of 1885, the loaded stage was ready to leave the Bluff Creek stop, which was five miles north of Runnels City. Early settlers C. N. Curry and C. E. Bell had run this stage stop since 1880. It was situated one mile southeast of present day Winters, Texas. As the driver popped his whip to start the team, the lead horse caused a commotion. As he bolted foreword, he pulled a buckle on the lines through one of the hame rings where it caught. Try as he might, the driver could not shake it loose. This horse on a short line turned the stage quickly as it made small circles. After a few rounds, the stage fell over hurting all the passengers except W. A. Wright of San Angelo who was riding on the outside.

Passengers cried and complained as they identified their cuts and scratches. Lottie Mitchell broke her arm, J.J. Corkery of St. Louis injured his spine, and John P. Sturgis of Taylor suffered a sprained ankle and bruised knee. The slightly injured included C.C. Parker of Abilene; J.F. Waters of St. Joe, Missouri; Thomas Aguilan; and Frank Lee.

The newspaper writer took up for the stage line when he explained that such an accident could happen any time. He felt the passengers should not blame the stage owners. In the same general area, Runnels County, a fire was reported on Fritz Karger's ranch. Some freighters with their wagons somehow started a hot blaze. Dry grass being abundant soon caused the fire to rage out of control. The news recorded the burned countryside to be six miles by eight miles wide.

While stages made their way to Abilene from San Angelo, they also passed through Colorado City, some 70 miles northwest of San Angelo. In the late 1800s there was a stage line from this town to Fort Sumner, New Mexico. One of the stage stops in this wide-open area was at a community called Durham, which was located on Bull Creek, some ten miles southeast of Gail. The station operators here in Borden County also ran a trading post.

Elizabeth Good rode a stage from Colorado City to Gail in 1896. As a sixteen-year old, her family allowed Elizabeth to board the T & P Railroad train from their home in Dallas and travel to Colorado City. From there she rode a stage to Gail to visit her brother, Frank Good.

Elizabeth later mentioned that on the stage trip two traveling salesmen were very talkative and rather "smart." Will Kincaid, the stage driver, came to her rescue. He stopped the stage and asked Elizabeth if she would like to ride up front with him so she could enjoy the view. She gladly made the change. They forded rivers where there were no bridges and bounced along the hills near Gail, but the stage made its way safely to the stage stop.

Elizabeth must have enjoyed talking to the young driver because she was to see him again. Will became her date while she visited Borden County. One Sunday,

Elizabeth remembered that Will took her walking around town. They visited the new Borden County Jail and were accidentally locked inside.

When Elizabeth rode the stage to Colorado City, she had a choice as to where her next destination would be. She could have ridden to Sterling City because a stage left Colorado City, traveled through Spade, which was 12 miles southwest, and made its way to Sterling City. Such a route was available as late as 1910.

Although Elizabeth could have visited New Mexico if she wanted to continue westward, other routes shuffled people around in the Panhandle region also. The large number of buffalo hunters and the need for forts caused that part of the Panhandle to develop quickly. Charles Rath and Bob Wright built a supply store on Sweetwater Creek in 1874. Their establishment became a part of Hidetown, which swelled to 150 citizens. Most of the dwellings were made of buffalo hide so the town's name was appropriate.

The next summer, Fort Elliott opened to protect the hunters and stage riders from Indians. Its location was near Mobeetie, which is near the present-day town of Pampa. Col. Nelson A. Miles established this campsite on the North Fork of the Red River. By January of 1875, 422 officers and men of the Fifth Infantry and Sixth Cavalry called this place home. As the years went by, a mail route developed from Mobeetie to Tascosa. This new connection allowed Mobeetie to be the commercial center of the region.

A. G. Springer was responsible for another stage route. In 1875 he built a trading post for buffalo soldiers, black army soldiers. His buildings were located where Boggy Creek emptied into the Canadian River in Hemphill County. Springer knew that Indians raided the area so he fortified his trading post so well that some men called it Fort Sitting Bull. Eventually there was enough traffic in his area that a stage went from Fort Elliott to Mobeetie. The horses stopped at Springer's Boggy Station.

Business went well for Springer so that he was named postmaster of that community in 1878. If he had stuck to stages and selling items to buffalo soldiers, he would have had a good business, but his station became a gambling joint also. After the cards flew about the table on November 17, 1878, a quarrel between gamblers erupted. Bullets zinged across the room. When the shooting was over, both Springer and his hired hand, Tom Ledbetter, were dead.

This community was where Thomas T. McGee registered his Quarter Circle C brand in 1883. A short time later he owned interest in the P O Ranch where he was foreman. McGee was well liked by the citizens of the area so he was elected Sheriff of Hemphill County. McGee and Vastine Stickley, his deputy, operated a wagon yard and livery stable in the town of Canadian until 1893.

This area seemed to calm down with the law so visible, but McGee would see more gunplay when the Wells Fargo safety box was transferred to the office one time. Gunshots rang out from a would-be robber. McGee died from a bullet he received in the battle.

Life was a bit calmer south of the Panhandle area. The Abilene to San Angelo stage made the newspaper regularly because change was coming. In June of 1885, the Abilene Stage Office moved to Harris Drug Store, and a year later, the line sold. Its new name was the Great Western Livery Stable. When the stage line changed hands, the new owners put up a new front on their business. Although some characteristics of the line might be new, the one stable part of the line was the employee named Eli Bates. According to a newspaper article, it was understood that the line could change hands, but Bates must continue his job and be in charge of the stages.

Another stage driver, W. J. Ellis, continued to live near San Angelo in the Harriet community after he could no longer pop his whip at the horses. The old man liked to visit and tell stories during Sunday School. In the small church of that area, the children's Sunday School was held in the back of the sanctuary while adults were seated near the front. As a young boy, Jay Farris said he liked to listen to Mr. Ellis during church because he could quote scriptures well. One saying the old stagecoach driver uttered was, "There's so much bad in everybody that you can't find much good in any of us." He may have had the stage robbers in his mind at that time.

Stage drivers in Central Texas never knew what challenges they would encounter next. In May of 1885, Will Jenkins drove a stage that crossed the San Saba River. The area above this crossing experienced torrential rains before Jenkins headed the stage down its southern route. He must not have realized the height of the raging water because his stage was swept away as soon as he started over the 10-mile crossing. Will was able to save only himself and one horse. The other horses drown as the mail floated down the river. Business transactions were lost in the mail, a

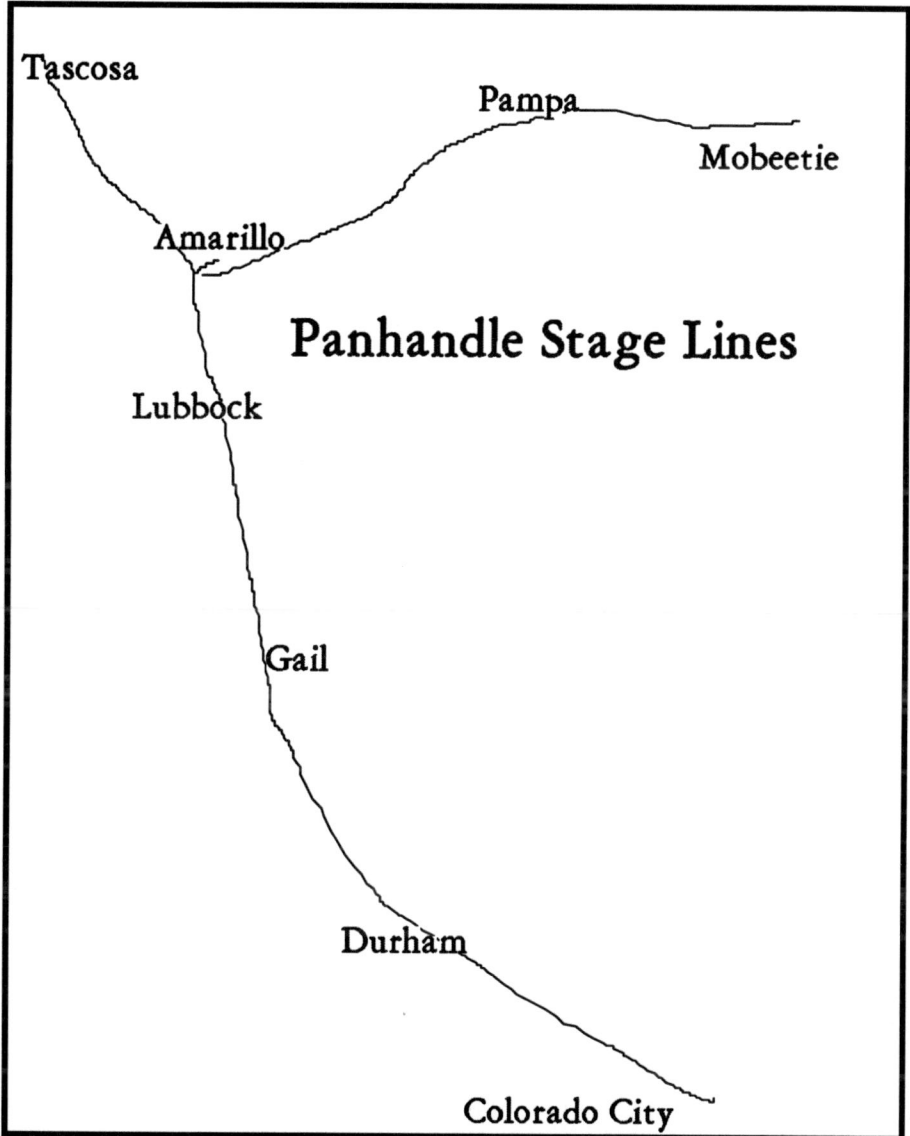

Tascosa

Pampa

Mobeetie

Amarillo

Panhandle Stage Lines

Lubbock

Gail

Durham

Colorado City

situation that brought inconvenience to some people.

Stage owners tried different things to encourage people to ride in their hacks. Although new schedules and connections added to the stage lines' ability to get passengers to ride them, the overhead of such an endeavor was hard on owners. In January of 1886, the San Angelo and Abilene Stage Line was purchased by the Southwestern Stage Company of Lawrence, Kansas. The new company wanted to attract more stage passengers, so they advertised that no charge would be made in its first month of business.

New ownership meant big changes in personnel. J. R. Barnett who was involved with the San Angelo and Abilene Stage Line for some time was not happy with the new ownership. He let it be known that he was leaving town for good. He indicated that he might return to California. Another man closely involved with the same stage Line was Eli Bates. He talked of leaving San Angelo also, but one newspaper writer thought that Bates' leaving would be a problem. He went so for as to print, "Some means needs to be used to keep Bates."

In January of 1886, there was much talk in the streets of San Angelo about a railroad coming to town. Some people saw this idea as good while others did not. The old stage driver, Eli Bates, complained about the iron rails and anything riding on them. As time passed though, he understood the progress the railroads brought to a town, so the press said, "Eli Bates has changed his tune and is howling for a railroad as loud as anybody."

Bates had driven the stage from San Antonio to El Paso when there were very few towns along the way. But when he was too old to drive, Bates continued working as manager of the stage line.

Most people in West Texas recognized him in his simple coat covering his large stomach, his flowing beard that reached his collar, and his pants stuffed into his boots. When the railroad replaced the stage, Bates moved away from the tracks. In 1888, he departed from San Angelo and lived in the nearby community of Ben Ficklin. By this time, a flood had washed most of Ben Ficklin away. Some of its businesses were rebuilt in San Angelo.

When Bates knew he would no longer drive a stage, he still owned an iron chest weighing about 200 pounds and measuring two feet long and 18 inches wide. It was used to haul payroll money from San Antonio to Fort Concho. Legend has it that Bates gave it to a local gunsmith.

While most men in West Texas received pay for the hard work they did, some men tried to find an easier way to riches. Two bankers and a stage driver, rather odd partners, held up a stage between Robert Lee and Ballinger on October 5, 1893. An examining trial for W. B. Buchanan, the president of the Coke County Bank; Charles Roe, the vice-president of the same bank, and John D. Walling, the stage driver; took place November 7, 1893 in San Angelo.

Deputy United States Marshall Broome arrested the three men at Robert Lee and brought them to San Angelo for the court procedure. Buchanan's bond was $12,000, Roe's $9,000 and Walling's only $4,000. The three defendants were to stand trial in El Paso's federal court in April, 1894. Unable to pay their bond, the three remained in jail.

Freighters rode the West Texas roads just as stage drivers did, although the chance of being robbed was much less for the freighter than the stage driver. Long before trains moved supplies from one part of Texas to another, freight wagons owned by hard working freighters brought dry goods and supplies to many remote mercantile stores. During the time that the stage transported people, and mail hacks moved the letters and packages from one town to another, men in Coke County freighted supplies from one town to another. William Latham and Walter Keenan, two independent freighters, often moved supplies from Robert Lee to San Angelo. After they journeyed the first day out of Robert Lee, they usually spent the night at a point called the Pecan Mott on the divide. The next night was spent at a wagon yard in San Angelo. The complete trip lasted four days.

As freighters moved about the countryside, they helped the economy of the area just like the stagecoach lines did. As Texas became more settled, stage lines spread throughout the once sparse West Texas country.

This Tom Green County Jail probably housed Coke County residents Charles Roe, W. B. Buchanan, and John D. Walling who held up a stage between Robert Lee and Ballinger. Photo was taken in 1884 by M. C. Ragdale and is courtesy of The West Texas Collection at Angelo State University.

Chapter 7: Other Stage Routes in Central Texas

Another stage owner who rivaled the accomplishments of John Butterfield was John T. Chidester. But to tell about his stagecoaches in Texas, one has to go back to Camden, Arkansas, to understand the whole story.

In 1857 John Chidester moved to Camden and established Chidester, Rapley and Company, which had a stage line. This business provided mail and stage service across South Arkansas, Northern Louisiana, and Texas. They also provided a four-horse team harnessed to nine-passenger coaches.

In 1862 Chidester bought a beautiful ten-roomed house that sat on a hill near Camden. This purchase, made with $10,000 in gold, included a large red barn where Chidester kept his many horses that he loved.

In the spring of 1864, federal troops attacked Chidester's house and searched for him. He was accused of rifling through the U. S. Mail to get Union secrets, which he gave to the Confederates. The troopers, dressed in blue, really wanted to nab this stagecoach owner, but Chidester hid among the trunks in a small attic room of his house and evaded the soldiers. When John Chidester felt it was safe to leave the house, he quickly departed to Texas.

After the war ended and Chidester received amnesty, he developed a long stage route from Fort Worth, Texas to Yuma, Arizona. His home was the central mail station of the Butterfield Overland Stage route in 1878. He employed 300 men, owned 2,000 horses, and 60 Concord coaches. Old hurts concerning the Civil War were a thing of the past because Chidester no longer feared the Union soldiers. In fact he had a detachment of the U. S. Army guarding his coaches along the roads in the West.

At his home, his two-storied barn was filled with both coaches and horses. He also used two upstairs rooms of his home for the stage drivers and any overnight passengers. His operation lasted only three years because the Texas and Pacific Railroad soon chugged through the southern states.

The Chidester Stage ran from Fort Worth to El Paso and San Francisco. One old timer mentioned traveling from Tucson to Fort Worth when forty miles was the normal limit the stage could make in one day. On these long trips, the stage traveled night and day, so most passengers took some food with them to eat. They didn't depend on the coach stopping for anything but horses.

The Chidester Stage Line used a buckboard from Tucson to Silver City, a four-horse stage to Ft. Concho, a buckboard to Coleman, and a four-horse stage to Fort Worth. From Ft. Hancock to Ft. Davis an escort of Negro soldiers accompanied them. This trip started December 17th and finished in Fort Worth January 21, 1878. Storms and bad weather slowed them down so that only twenty days were actually used for riding the stage. The fare for this journey from Tucson to Fort Worth was $240 not including meals.

Many small stage lines in Central Texas fed into the larger line headed to El Paso. One such coach came through Sipe Springs, a town 25 miles northwest of Comanche, Texas. The first settlers who stopped their wagons in this area came in 1873. Within the next ten years, the community had a schoolhouse as well as a post office. When the early occupants of the town noticed water seeping along the nearby branch, they named the town after the springs.

Some people thought the spelling should be "Seep Springs," while others thought it should be "Seap," but most of the citizens leaned toward the spelling "Sipe." When a name couldn't be decided upon, Cal Watkins found a dictionary that said "Sipe" with two dots over the "i" sounded the same as the other two spellings, so that point dictated the naming of the community. In 1884, 140 people called Sipe Springs home. Buildings such as two hotels, five general stores and two gin-gristmills made the community look like a real town.

In March of 1876, W. B. Johnson owned the stage line between Waco and Comanche. He often rode the stage to Comanche, so a newspaper writer of the *Comanche Chief* described the stage owner's disposition. He mentioned that Johnson was "irrepressible John, who comes rain or shine, epizootic or no 'zootic.'" Johnson must have had a sense of humor since he was known to lift everybody's spirits.

The tiny town of Sipe Springs enjoyed its day as a stage stop. The Arkansas, Texas & Pacific Line was a stagecoach line owned by Col. John T. Chidester. His coach brought people from Fort Worth's train stations to this Central Texas town. The line was celebrated as one of the longest lines in the West because it went all the way from Central Texas through West Texas to Fort Yuma, Arizona.

In 1879, Sipe Springs received their mail daily from a stage passing through Eastland, and F. K. Stamey was the Sipe Springs postmaster. This stage route from

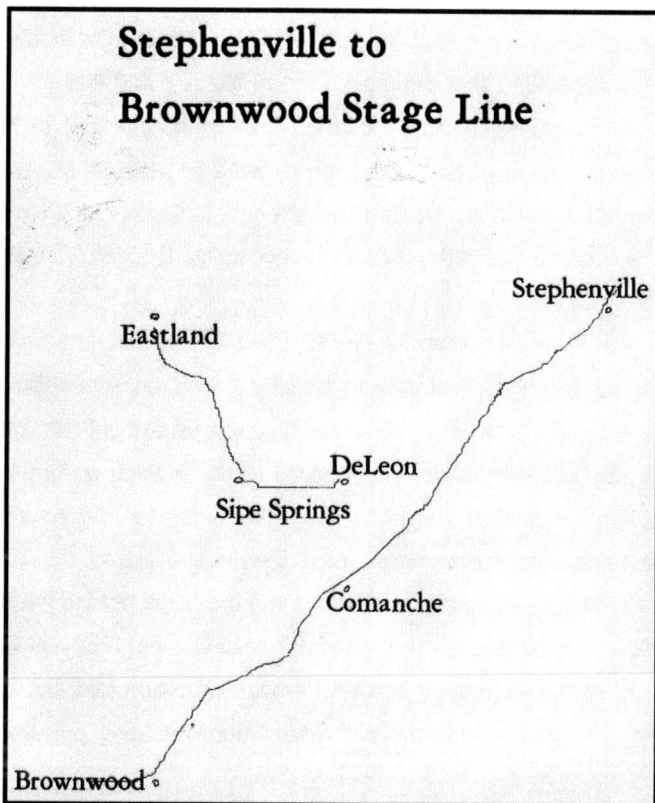

Stephenville to Brownwood Stage Line

Eastland started in 1878. J. A. Holman of Comanche was a relay driver whose route was from Brownwood to Stephenville. At this time, Sipe Springs needed a stage stop, so stage owner Chidester asked a favor from his friend, Capt. J. F. Childress. Soon the stages were stopping at Childress' house, which occasionally took on the identity of a hotel.

Sipe Springs residents witnessed an unusual event in the summer of 1889, when the soldiers from Fort Concho were moved to Fort Sill. Fort Concho had long been the home of the proud "Buffalo Soldiers." Their name came from the fact that Indian warriors admired the fighting ability of the black troopers, so they named them "Buffalo Soldiers" because their hair was curly like the buffalo. A group of black soldiers marched through the town of Sipe Springs while the stage carried the wives and children belonging to the troopers. Comanche county had no black people at that time, so the procession of soldiers was impressive.

At this time, citizens of Comanche received their mail from the Sipe Springs post office. Although Chidester kept the horses moving through Comanche County, by June of 1879, he predicted that the main office of the A T & P Mail Co. would move their stables and shop. He thought the other town would probably be Stephenville. When Chidester cut his route to 13 days, he received an increase in pay, which was somewhat unusual. Until 1881, the train brought mail to Comanche three times a day although Yuma, Arizona mail made it to town once a day. By 1881, Comanche County had eight post offices.

One stage line in Comanche County came from DeLeon to Sipe Springs, a distance of about 16 miles. According to Dorothy Robertson, when the stage came down Main Street in the Sipe Springs community, it moved straight through town. This coach, called the Chidester Stage Line, stopped at the seeping springs to water the horses. This location marked the main source of water for the community. After watering the team, the driver maneuvered the horses across the street to the Childress Inn. At this point, he changed horses and the stage headed westward where it would eventually pass through El Paso and Yuma, Arizona. Although the Childress Inn was built in 1874, eventually it burned. Dorothy Robertson said that south of Sipe Springs, there are ruts in the rocky road toward the Armstrong property where the stage passed.

Probably the stage left Sipe Springs and stopped at a stage stand north of Brownwood Airport called Salt Creek. There was a stage station there at one time. This location is west of Highway 183 between May and Brownwood.

Some buildings in Sipe Springs had dual purposes. One such structure was owned by C. L. Taylor. His saloon was in the front portion and for a time, the rear portion of the building was used as ten-pin alley. When heavy balls no longer knocked over the pins, this area changed to a stable. The Arkansas, Texas & Pacific Mail Company used it as a place to keep their horses.

Sometime after midnight on a cold Friday night in January of 1881, flames of fire shot out of the stable. Eight stage horses, tied inside the building, were helpless. Onlookers said the fire was aided by strong winds blowing as well as several barrels of whiskey present in the building. All the horses were lost as well as harnesses and sacks of feed.

Mr. Taylor had not used the saloon portion of the building for quite awhile, but some observers thought the fire was arson. According to the local news, a similar blaze was set a short time before this incident at the nearby gin of Mr. Spinks. Mr. Taylor estimated the contents of the saloon were worth $800, the building worth $500, and the horses and equipment worth $1,000. Taylor owned an insurance policy on the building worth $1,000, but he knew it would be short of the total loss he estimated at $2,500. Some people felt that the fire hastened the end of the Sipe Springs stagecoach run because it was cancelled after this incident.

Some stagecoaches passing through the Comanche County area could have looked similar to this Well-Fargo stage owned by Truett Auldridge of Goldthwaite. Author's Collection.

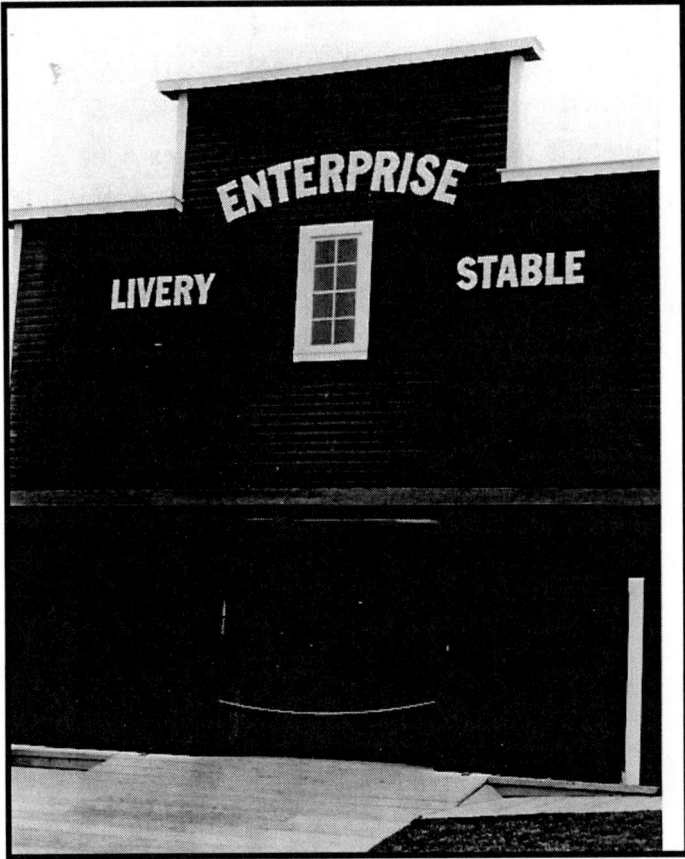

This livery stable might have been similar to the one used in Sipe Springs. Such buildings often had more than one use like the one did in that community. Author's collection.

Chapter 8: Freighters

Many Texans in the 1800s made their living as freighters, sitting long hours on their wagons as they moved between communities and homesteads. They carried farming equipment, furs, household goods, and even heavy woolsacks in their "prairie schooner" wagon. This particular wagon was built to stand the wear and tear of the mountainous regions of far West Texas, so they wouldn't win many races, but they'd stay together.

Some of the larger four thousand-pound wagons had a twenty-four feet long bed that was four and a half feet wide. The fact that the sides were five and a half feet high made the wagon appear top-heavy when the wagon bows were in place with a two-piece tarpaulin attached. The wagon was higher than it was wide. But when ten or more mules were hitched to pull a good-sized load, the schooner swayed from side to side. This gave the mules a break as it weaved back and forth.

The wheels were large even though they didn't compare to the two-wheeled ox-cart wheel. The schooner had five feet, ten inch hind wheels and front wheels that were positioned twelve inches lower. The brake to hopefully stop these wheels was made of a seven-foot beam that was six by eight inches square. When a driver applied the brakes, this beam pressed against the wheels.

Long before trains moved supplies from one part of Texas to another, freight wagons driven by hard working men brought dry goods and supplies to many remote Texas mercantile stores. Most of these drivers owned their wagons and hauled seasonally. When springtime descended on West Texas, most ranchers had sheep with thick wool. As shearing season came, freighters headed their wagons to the ranches of West Texas, usually loaded with supplies for the rancher. On the return trip, their wagons were piled high as they drove to the larger towns with bulging woolsacks. When fencing pastures became a necessity, fence posts found their way into the freighter's wagons.

Strangely enough during the 1870s, many buffalo killed in Texas became huge piles of bones, thanks to the bone collectors. Freighters hitched two or more wagons together to haul the sun-bleached bones to the nearest railroad. Ranchers who were done-in by the drought, also collected bones with the help of their wife and children. Income from this venture kept the wolf of hunger away from their door for a little while longer.

A wool train ready to leave San Angelo, Texas in 1911. Central National Bank Building is in the background. Courtesy of West Texas Collection, Angelo State University.

The freighters who hauled flour, sugar, beans, and other supplies from Kansas to Texas forts needed a load of something to sell on their return trip. They found another commodity when these bone piles bleached enough that they were easy to pick up. Areas of the Panhandle near the Arkansas River proved to be the first good source of bones. About the time that freighters decided to pick up bones, the Atchison, Topeka and the Santa Fe Railway inched its way into Texas.

Freighters had ingenuous ways of hooking three wagons together and pulling the load of bones across the plains. Early settlers mentioned as many as one hundred wagons of bones they saw at one time making a caravan to the nearest railroad. The freighters dumped the bones and identified each pile in such as way that the railroad workers knew who owned the piles.

Some freighters represented grocery companies and peddled their wares over West Texas. Arthur Albert, born August 17, 1878 in Denton, Texas, decided to move to San Angelo in 1898. At first he worked as a salesman for Temple Grocery Company. The route he made included Sherwood, Stiles, Ozona, Girvin, Buena Vista, Ft. Stockton, Del Rio, and Menardville. When he departed on this trip, he expected to be gone two or three weeks.

Freighter A. A. Glover was related to the Phillip Walker family of Mertzon, Texas. Phillip said, "Glover hugged the hills as he drove from Sherwood to Stiles." He explained that the wagons maneuvered over the flatter areas instead of climbing the hills like the road does today.

A stone marker has been discovered west of Sherwood on the J. T. Davis ranch. Phillip says this marker has two arrows and two towns on it. One arrow points to Stiles and the other to Sherwood.

When the freighters, often called drummers, stayed away from home for a long trip, they were anxious to visit with other drummers. Glover mentioned that he liked to meet the other freighters at a windmill near the present site of Barnhart, Texas.

John A. Menges, a freighter from Menard, actually used the oxcart instead of a wagon to carry provisions between towns and forts in West Texas. He knew some of the soldiers stationed at Fort Mason such as General George Custer. Menges heard Custer complaining that he never had been able to kill a deer while in the Texas Hill Country. Menges took time off from his freighting duties to take the soldier on deer hunts. He explained to Custer how to track the deer and how to find them. The two hunters became good friends, and Menges said he would have followed the General toward the northwest except that he was ill when Custer left Fort Mason.

Bustling West Texas towns were a sight to behold. The freighters directing their wagons and carts were always a noisy site. These first teamsters driving ox teams could be easily heard as they shouted, "whoa, gee, or haw" wherever they were. When there were supplies to haul, the streets were crowded with ox-driven rigs as well as horse and mule driven. This caused lots of congestion, cussing drivers, popping whips, and braying mules. Twelve animals might be pulling two or three wagons hooked together down the middle of the street. Tempers flared and mishaps occurred, but amazingly they had few bad wrecks.

A picture of Fort Mason reconstructed on the original site overlooking the town of Mason. Many of the stage stops centered around existing forts such as this one, and freighters stopped there as well. Author's Collection.

Each wagon master had wooden bows mounted on his wagon so wagon sheets could be stretched in case of rain. The freight rig wasn't complete unless it had a plunder cart attached to the last wagon. This smaller wagon held horse feed, grub, bedding, cooking stuff, and harness repair tools. One wagon usually had a water barrel lashed on the side. Some freighters carried large watering buckets for their team. These containers were needed because most seasoned drivers found it easier to carry water to the team instead of unhooking the harness and leading the horses to the river.

Orland Sims lived to see the teams of freighters visiting his ranch home near Paint Rock and maneuvering their wagons in towns like San Angelo. Sims described the arrangement of the horses in a team in his book *Cowpokes, Nesters, & So Forth*:

Most teams were hooked two abreast with the largest, strongest animals, known as wheelers, in the rear. Then come the swing teams, and finally the leaders. The wheelers and the leaders were the important members of the team, for upon their strength and intelligence depended the smooth operation of the rig. A bronc could be tied close to his gentle teammate, and there was nothing much that he could do except to go along with the team.

Drivers didn't always sit on the seat of the wagon. If they had three teams or more, the driver preferred to ride the near wheeler horse. He had a rope connected to a long brake lever so he could control the brakes on the lead wagon. If the brakes failed, trouble developed with the wagon hitting the heels of the team. An expert driver could keep the wagon away from the team and could use a single jerk line to control many horses or mules. The driver also carried a sack of small rocks that he could expertly bounce off the rump of a horse that was slowing down too much.

Freighters traveled in all kinds of weather. Sometimes their wagons bounced over barely visible trails, which turned to a mud hole in rainy times. The bogged down wagons not only slowed other traffic trying to pass their way but also left the towns with short supply of groceries when they got stuck. Freighters had to get the goods through, no matter flood or dust storm.

Reynaldo Camunez was a freighter during the early 1880's in the Saint Angela area. He probably knew most of the ranchers and merchants in West Texas. Reynaldo fell in love with a German lady named Otilia Markwardt who came to this area with a small daughter named Kate. They came from the Fredericksburg area, and she accompanied the Taylor family from that community to the Ben Ficklin area, near San Angelo. She continued to work for the Taylors in their new home. Otilia could only speak German, and her boyfriend could only speak Spanish, but different languages didn't keep them apart. They were married in 1881.

Reynaldo and his wife lived near Ben Ficklin when the Flood of 1882 swept through. Otilia, was working for Mrs. Elizabeth Taylor at the Bismarck Farm at the time the waters began to rise. Otilia and her small daughter, Kate, waded to safety. Reynaldo decided to switch from farming to freighting soon after the flood. To this family were added the following children:

Reynaldo, Jr., Frank, Lola, Emilia, Angelita and Maria. Their father died in 1887 from a hemorrhage of the lungs. In the early 1900's, young

Reynaldo Camunez freighted fence wire and other materials for people in West Texas. Courtesy of the West Texas Collection, Angelo State University.

Reynaldo Jr. took up the freighting business also with eight mules and two wagons.

He remarked that the freighting business was hard, slow work. The roads were so bad that it would take him half a day to go from Saint Angela to the Twin Mountains, a distance of about ten miles. If the trip took more than a day, Reynaldo slept under his wagon and ate from his chuck box. When his business grew enough to have two wagons, his other driver would meet him half way with an empty wagon. They then exchanged wagons so Reynaldo could load the empty one in town and make ready for a new trip.

Reynaldo hauled to nearby ranches and merchants in small towns. The ranchers needed building materials, wire, posts, cattle feed, gasoline, and groceries. He hauled as far as Mason, Sonora, Ozona, Pecos, and Marfa. Sonora seemed to need a lot of beer. Reynaldo told stories about taking many five-ton loads of beer to that town. He also remembered hauling the first drilling rig to the Key Ranch in Tom Green County.

Besides having a hot, dusty job, Mexican freighters met some opposition with white freighters who called themselves the "White Funion." A person could surmise that "F" stood for "freighters." At that time, Mexican freighters moved a lot of wagons down the trails of West Texas, and they were very dependable. An

Hannigan's Freight Service wagon at Fort Chadbourne. Picture taken by author April, 2005.

unusually threatening letter was sent to the Mexican freighters and was reprinted in the *San Angelo Standard*, March 24, 1894. It said the following:

NotiFied Not to loAD Any MoRE MeXicAn WaGons With FreiGht AfteR MARch the 20. IF yoU Do you Will Bee SWinGeD oUt of toWN and noT
Too a GOOD Spot to BilD. WriGht Otion SA Gelo SoNoRa OZoNo. ThiS iS to sHeePMeN too Not to LoDE thEm WitH woOl or hIt wiLL Bee BURnt AnY mAN LoADinG meXiCaN WAGonS Will LooS his FReiGht AnD Bee BURn out if You lodE AnYmoRe meXiCAn WAgOmS YoU maY LooK to Bee BURnt oUT iF AnY SheeP meN LoAD theM theY WiLLGit theRe WoOL BURnt.
          WhitE FUnioN

The Standard editor said, "The following threatening letter evidently written by some white freighter for the purpose of intimidation has been received by several merchants of this city. As Mexicans do nearly two thirds of the hauling of this section and are among the most reliable and careful freighters we have, the threat has fallen on very deaf ears."

Ranchers were often their own freighters and would go to town once or twice a year for supplies. Sometimes a ranch hand drove the wagon and the ranch family went to town in style. They'd move along faster in a buggy or hack while the wagon trailed behind.

Some freighters worked alone and only when seasonal work came along did they hitch up the freight wagon for a trip. Dave Gentry lived in Sherwood, 25 miles southwest of San Angelo. He delivered salt to ranchers in the spring and brought their clips of wool back from the ranch after shearing. Ranchers instructed him as to where he should leave the wool.

Once he took his wife and youngest children along for the trip to a ranch some sixty miles southwest of Sherwood. Along the way back home, they passed through Ozona where his wife shopped for the children. The whole family jumped out of the wagon and headed for the mercantile store. They needed shoes for the children and material for Dave's wife to make clothes. When the trip was nearly over, his wife asked how much he made on the haul. Dave asked, "How much did you spend on the children's shoes and material?" When she answered, Dave said, "Well, we just about broke even." Maybe she wasn't invited to go on the next trip.

If a freighter made it to a fair sized town before dark, he camped in a wagon yard. Wagon yards took the place of hotels, which some travelers could afford and others couldn't. Such a yard would cover a quarter of a city block. The larger ones were a whole block in size. They usually had several sheds, and hay boxes for the horse's feed were scattered about the many small pens. A fancy wagon yard had covered sheds where freighters could drive their wagons under them and protect their load from bad weather. The small sheds were used for the wagon drivers and their families to camp for the night.

The wagon yard grounds were one extreme or the other. It was either covered with several inches of manure, straw, and dust or soggy with recent rains. Six inches of mud mixed with the distinct smell of manure, sweaty horses, and harness gear wouldn't be exactly where you'd want to lay your bedroll.

Some wagon yards had no sheds, so the ground was where you put your

S. M. Oglesby Feed and Wagon Yard in Sherwood 1906. Photo is courtesy of Irion County Historical Society.

bedroll. A tarpaulin covered your bedding so none of the moisture seeped inside.

The freighter's kitchen was in the same location. At night one could view many little campfires glowing near the parked wagons. A freighter usually cooked coffee, bacon, and beans for himself. As he looked out over the horses in the pens, he probably saw collar galls on the horse's shoulders and bare red places on their flanks where the traces rubbed. Some horses were drawn and stood with heads hung low, if they'd been pushed too hard that day.

Emigrants and other traveling families lived in the same environment. Hotels were expensive and not always available so even the ranch families who came to town camped in the wagon yard. The owner of the wagon yard charged a fee of about 25 cents per team, which included feed for the animals. However, the driver had to unharness and feed the horses himself.

The first wagon yards in San Angelo were probably the Elkhorn Wagon Yard on Concho Street, just west of Chadbourne Street, and the Girdwood's Wagon Yard, which was east of Oakes Street. During Cleveland's administration, wool sold as low as four cents a pound, sheep brought fifty cent to a dollar a head, and cattle brought less than ten dollars each so most ranchers didn't have much money to spend on a hotel.

Some of the successful ranchers continued to camp in the wagon yards even when they had enough money to buy the complete hotel building. Habits were hard to break. One would think that they must have liked the camaraderie of visiting with other ranchers and freighters in the wagon yards.

Some wagon yards changed hands rather frequently. Si Merchant sold the Elk Horn to John Guest. Hughes Bros. bought this elite wagon yard and finally sold it to James W. Johnson. Mr. Johnson said two shootings took place in the Elk Horn. One happened at the back of the yard in the black of night. A woman came into the yard with a teamster and was supposedly the reason for the gun-play. In the other incident, a man followed a second man from Temple, Texas to San Angelo. Shots rang out, first on the north side of Concho Avenue, as the chase developed across the street, and then the fatal shot was fired near the Coney Island Saloon.

Jim Johnson told how early cowboys loved to play tricks on green horns who came their way. Arthur West was a young man who around 1900 left his horse at the Elk Horn. The man on duty asked the city slicker-looking young fellow if he had a gun. West said he didn't so the man gave him a big six-shooter to ram under his belt.

As West started across Concho Avenue, a cowboy carrying two guns stopped him and said, "Hello, young man, I'm the sheriff. Do you have a gun?" West nodded yes and pulled the gun from under his belt. The cowboy took the gun and ushered West to the saloon.

"Look here boys, what I took off this man," the acting-sheriff said. "What'll we do with him?"

"Shoot him," said one of the gang, "and throw him in the river."

"With a weight to his neck," said another.

"I tell you what," said the acting-sheriff, "We'll let him off with a round of drinks." West seemed relieved to get off with just a ten-dollar bar tab, and when the pretend-sheriff offered him his gun back, West said he didn't need it.

The wagon yard in Mason, Texas, always had an influx of cowboys immediately after a big herd had been sold, and the cowboys received their pay in gold. When nightfall came, the cowboys threw their bags of gold in a safe place under the chuckwagon and played poker near the campfires. This activity usually lasted most of the night.

As more people moved to West Texas, the number of wagon yards increased. About 1910, San Angelo had as many as eight yards in use at the same time. The automobile made its presence around 1912 so that by 1918, San Angelo only had three yards in use. By 1929 the Elkhorn Wagon Yard was the only one in existence. This yard catered to truckers and shearing crews. Roads were better and nearly every family had a car of some kind. The Elkhorn discontinued in 1943 and a filling station was put in its place.

Freighter's lives were solitary, and they found entertainment wherever they could. Will Pool was hauling a load of salt to the Harris Brother's ranch near Stiles in Reagan County. After he delivered his load, he made camp close to the community of Stiles. He hobbled his horses and went to the dance at the local dance hall. Later that night, he returned to camp and slept. He jumped out of his bedroll during the night because a skunk bit him. Will returned to San Angelo within a few days, but he continued to worry about the bite.

"Maybe the skunk was carrying rabies," he thought. When the freighter got a chance, he went to a woman who had special powers. When he explained the bite to the healer, she treated the wound with a madstone. It's a puffy stone that is found in a deer's stomach. She boiled it first and then laid the warm rock on Will's wound. It was left there fourteen hours, heated again, and returned to the wound. Friends say that Will suffered no bad experiences from the wound, or the treatment.

A freight route between Bronte and Ballinger was also popular. Doll Best kept his horses moving over this road. Since G. L. Bridges owned a hardware store, he freighted much of his inventory between Bronte and Ballinger. Willis L. McCraw began freighting when he lived in Comstock. Later he moved to Coke County and continued to use his horses and wagons to move supplies. He ran his wagons between Robert Lee, Bronte, and San Angelo. Willis managed to farm between his freight jobs.

As early as the 1870 Coke County Census, the name Thomason appeared on the roll. James Turner Thomason was one family member who preferred the far western part of the state of Texas. He managed to climb over the border and land in New Mexico where he freighted goods from his home to El Paso. With a successful garden, he was able to pick potatoes and cabbages, which along with his wife's hand-churned butter, he traded in El Paso. Thomason came home with sugar, flour, and soap in 100 bar boxes. He was an example of a person who freighted with his covered wagon and made a good living.

Most families who came to town in their wagon on a trip planned to stay overnight in a wagon yard. Some of the freighters also pulled their wagons inside the protected corral. Wagons were lined up so each person had enough space for a fire. Children scampered among the wagons and met new friends while their mother cooked over the fire. Adults visited with other travelers in the nearby wagons so they could hear the latest news. In the dusk, campfires flickered all over the yard. Men unhitched their teams and lead the horses or mules to a nearby pen.

One woman knew quite a bit about wagon yards. Helen Lamborn carried the distinction of being born in the Elkhorn Wagon Yard while her father owned this business in 1886. Helen married J. Van Ketchum in 1935, and he died soon afterward. Mrs. Ketchum was quoted as saying, "The name of the Elkhorn wagon yard came from the fact that a stuffed moose's head was mounted in the wagon yard office." She also explained that staying in the wagon yard in the late 1800s was equivalent to staying in a hotel today.

One businessman owned a wagon yard so he could use wagons to help disperse his dry goods. John Abe March had a dry goods store next to a wagon yard that took care of freighters whom he hired to distribute his goods in West Texas. He and his brothers came to San Angelo in 1890. John March arrived in the San Angelo area first as a doctor, but he soon entered the trading business. N.M. March took charge of the dry goods department, Bishop March the grocery business, and S. W. March Sr. took over the management of the office. Brother Murphy March handled their ranch enterprises.

The brothers built up a large trading center and needed many freighters to ship their goods. Early in the morning at the back of the March Brothers' Store, big freight wagons, pulled by six or eight teams of horses, waited to be loaded from their docks. People estimated that the brothers ran a half-million dollar business annually. Their freight wagons traveled as far as Juno, Texas, while delivering goods.

Often times the March Brothers' wagons hauled wool back to town. The firm purchased wool on commission. Sometimes they sold it on a high market of 72.5 cents and sometimes they sold it as low as 11 cents. They battled the droughty years with their patrons, and financed the start of many a ranch.

The March Brothers were an icon of West Texas businesses, but even they had to close their doors for one final time on January 1, 1939.

Some men such as John Guest didn't own equipment or supplies to be hauled by wagons, but they owned wagon yards strictly as a business. When Guest bought the Elkhorn Wagon Yard, he added bunkhouses for the freighters and stalls for the animals. The Hughes Brothers bought the Elite Wagon Yard and later sold it to James W. Johnson. Johnson explained that both funny and tragic things happened around the yards. People visited after they put up their horses and often played jokes on any tenderfoot who came along. They also got in squabbles and fights.

These men helped D. E. Cocreham with his stage and freight teams. Mr. Cocreham's grandson, James Elder, believed the freight yard was in the 200 or 300 block of 3rd Street in San Angelo. Picture is courtesy of James Elder.

D. E. Cocreham employed quite a few hands to keep his stages operating. He also ran a freight yard in San Angelo. W. H. Parsons of Uvalde, Texas, remembered bringing his wagon into the old Daggett Wagon Yard in San Antonio during the 1880s. He said, "We get in there, maybe in time to get around and buy our stuff, but we never loaded out till the next day." Parsons explained that he loved to eat supper in an actual restaurant that night and check out the town, but he would always sleep at his wagon so he could get an early start the next day. About daylight everybody in the wagon yard was rattling their coffee pot and skillet because they had to eat breakfast a long time before the restaurants opened.

Parsons said that the Doak Bowles wagon yard was one of the early yards in Uvalde. Travelers who camped in the wagon yards loved to play jokes on unassuming people. One such insurance salesman was sucked into the story of several men who had a badger hidden in a sack. They had a rope attached to the badger. A huge dog standing nearby was to battle the badger. Some men bet on the dog and others bet on the badger. When the insurance salesman was asked to pull on the rope to let the badger out, a big commode jar full of beer, coffee grounds and ginger snaps appeared. Then the insurance salesman knew he was the brunt of the joke.

When men weren't playing jokes on people in the wagon yard, they were likely trading something. Many a horse was offered for trade, usually a worn out one that was poor and had its ribs showing. Women got into the trading also because they brought eggs, vegetables, bacon, lard, and pecans to trade. These purchases and trades made in the wagon yards seemed to be the prelude to later trade days and markets found in many communities today.

In 1898 Mrs. Paul Wilson of Medina said that she drove one wagon full of hogs to San Antonio while her husband drove a second wagon. When they received the money at the slaughter yards for the hogs, Mrs. Wilson said that her husband had enough cash to buy a brand new Studebaker wagon. Of course they stayed at the Fest Wagon Yard for the night.

Some wagon teams had their own ideas according to Mrs. Wilson. One time her husband had their wagon loaded and ready to leave the Schreiner Wagon Yard in Kerrville. Mr. Wilson was ready to go, so he jumped off the wagon to open the gate at the yard. Before he could grab the reins, the horses bolted through the gate and down the streets of Kerrville with no driver. After running five or six miles, the horses crossed the Guadalupe River and Town Creek. The team was headed home to Medina and they made it to the top of twelve-mile hill before a man stopped them. Luckily for the Wilsons, nothing was lost.

Settlers like Berry Buckelew became a freighter only when the need arose. He lived on the Sabinal River in Bandera County in 1866. The homesteads were few and far between at that time, so each man took his turn to drive his wagon on the long trip to San Antonio periodically for supplies.

Buckelew drove the older styled ox wagon with huge wheels. He pulled it with five oxen yoked together. To make the trip profitable, he stopped at a shingle camp on the Medina and loaded his wagon with Cypress shingles. The workers cut many shingles from one of the huge Cypress trees growing on the riverbank.

After Buckelew sold his shingles for the customary price, he loaded his wagon with goods for his family and his neighbors. The return trip took several days, but his arrival was nearly as exciting as a trip to the store for everybody in the area.

Some wagon trains endured the lonely, isolated trails of far West Texas. Fort Lancaster guarded the trail from Ozona that headed to the Mexican border, some one hundred miles south. This outpost, located one mile northeast of where Live Oak Creek flows into the Pecos River, saw mule trains of twelve or more wagons. The wagon train boss was responsible for about 150 mules since each wagon used ten mules to pull over this rough area. The mountain trails were steep. Most mule trains also had twenty or so well-armed men for protection.

Live Oak Creek did its part to entice visitors to stop and rest awhile before tackling the trail to Horsehead Crossing on the Pecos. This stream had good water with fish in abundance. Firewood and shelter came from the ancient oaks along the stream so the soldiers saw quite a few visitors in the Fort Lancaster area.

Wagon trains also left Texas headed to Mexico. August Santleban, the man who ran the early-day stages along the Mexican border, also freighted south of the border. In 1876 he carried 350,000 pounds in silver and 40,000 pounds of copper from Chichuachua, Mexico into Texas. He came across the Rio Grande at Presidio and passed through Fort Davis, then San Antonio, and finally stopped at Indianola on the Gulf Coast.

Wagon trains were the prelude to the big trucks seen on the highways today, but the driver's life was a bit different with wagon yards and ranchers to contend with.

Some wagons seen traveling down the same roads as the stagecoaches and freighters used were of the two-wheeled variety. They required less horses. In fact, some men could pull their cart by themselves.

Some wagons used to haul water were of the two-wheeled variety. One horse could manage the load. This picture shows the early water-works of some towns in West Texas.

Chapter 9: Robbers on the Stage Routes

Just as passengers depended on the stages traveling east from San Angelo, the robbers did also. W. J. Ellis drove stages westward to El Paso for many years, but by the 1880s, he chose shorter routes to drive, such as the one between San Angelo and Abilene. Much to Ellis' dismay, he experienced robberies many times on this road. He also had other visitors.

In later years, Mr. Ellis liked to tell about the Indians he met along the trails. He witnessed a strange meal one day when he noticed some Indians putting axle grease on their crackers before eating them. These warriors often followed freighters across the prairie and obviously thought the grease that the teamsters carried in their wagons should be good for something.

Although Indians no longer attacked the stages in this region, somebody forgot to tell the robbers it was time to quit also. During the winter months of 1884, customers traveling on the stage between San Angelo and Abilene heard the words, "Stop and throw down your money" seven times. Some passengers hated to ride that route for fear of a holdup. Gen Grierson, commander of Fort Concho, refused to ride the stage between these two towns because there was so many holdups along the way.

Stagecoach driver Ellis remembered the names of two of the bandits, McDaniel and Potter, as he explained their exploits. He said they often camped at the edge of San Angelo near the Girdwood Wagon Yard. Ellis described the scenario of the robbery as the following: the stage left San Angelo about four in the morning headed toward Ballinger. McDaniel and Potter rode ahead and positioned themselves about six miles east of town. Stagecoach driver Ellis said they held the stage up as regular as clockwork. He described them as two people "Collecting their customary revenue."

Ellis remembered one holdup as a bit more unusual than the rest. On a cold, wintry day the two fellows, McDaniel and Potter, held up his stage while he was traveling east. The robbers knew that another stage driver, Davis, would travel the same road going west and be in their area soon. When Ellis left the scene of the robbery, they told him to tell the westbound stage to hurry because they were cold and did not want to wait so long. After 30 minutes of driving eastward, Ellis met Davis' westbound stage and relayed the robbers' message.

When the westbound stage met the two robbers, it stopped, and the robbers demanded jewelry and valuables from the seven passengers. Miss Annie Dixon, a passenger in the stage, had $1.50 hidden in her glove, but they stole it. When McDaniel and Potter found a very small amount of money on her person, they told Miss Dixon they would search her trunk. She said, "There is nothing in it but clothes."

William James Ellis drove the stage lines both near and far from San Angelo and experienced a lot of holdups. Courtesy of West Texas Collection, Angelo State University.

The robbers were so mad they cursed their bad luck and started to leave. The young woman actually had $75 hidden there, which she successfully retained.

Ellis said later to a reporter, "There were two officers on board the stage on this trip, when it was held up by Potter and McDaniel." He described one man as a deputy from a northern county and the other one was a U. S. Marshal from New Mexico. When the robbers asked for their valuables, the lawmen pulled their guns. The robbers opened fire first and shot one deputy in the chest. When the guns began to fire, the stage horses took off running. Potter and McDaniel, standing outside the stage, pumped their Winchesters at the fleeing stage, but it did not stop. The driver thought he had some fatalities for sure among his passengers due to the way the bullets whizzed by.

Two bullets did manage to pass through the overcoats of the driver and a ranchman named Edgar Stillson. This rancher rode on the boot along side the driver. Another bullet passed through Miss Dixon's trunk and penetrated the U. S. Marshall's back. Once the stage stopped in San Angelo, someone called Dr. S. L. S. Smith. He treated the deputy first because his back injury looked bad. However, the bullet used all its strength passing through the trunk and flattened on the lower end of the deputy's backbone. The marshal was not hurt badly. Mr. Stillson was not as fortunate because he was dead by the time they got around to examining his wound.

Potter and McDaniel hit town almost as soon as the stage did and had a good time discussing their exploits to whoever would listen at Pete King's Saloon. Although they were not caught for that robbery, a later holdup at Crow's Nest had different results. That particular time the stage, filled with Stutz's variety troupe, carried five women and six men with little cash. The robbers who were disappointed at such little success decided to take jewelry from the women, even though most of it was of cheap quality.

McDaniel eventually gave the stolen jewelry to his sweetheart who was living with her father in a sheep camp in Coke County. His girlfriend was Mr. Potter's sister. When her uncle visited the sheep camp, she showed him the jewelry, and he commented on the recent robbery. He did not know that his nephew stole the jewelry, but his knowledge of the jewelry later brought about the arrest of McDaniel and Potter.

Once the bandits were safely behind bars, Deputy U. S. Marshall T. J. Loring rode from San Antonio to San Angelo to summon witnesses. In October of 1884, Loring took W. H. Brown, Hal Young, and Hillis Bright with him to be a part of the state's case against Potter and McDaniel.

The two stagecoach robbers were tried in San Antonio and given fifty years in prison. It wasn't very long before McDaniel escaped from the San Antonio jail and rode toward his father's home in Kendall County. The law intercepted him between his home and a live oak thicket. McDaniel would not give up as he began firing at the officers. They returned the fire enough to break his right arm and one leg. The broken bones did not change McDaniel's attitude as he continued to shoot at the officers. They finally ended the stand off by shooting him in the head.

One time a young man was accused of robbing a stage that the well-known outlaw Rube Burris actually robbed. An area between San Angelo and Ballinger had been the scene of such robberies committed by Rube many times. The outlaw stopped the stage about fifteen miles from Ballinger. The masked man picked a stage carrying two preachers to apprehend. After the passengers were relieved of their valuables, and they reached a town that had a sheriff, one of the preachers said he knew the robber. He described him as a certain man he knew who was tall with a gray mustache. The lawmen captured the suspect fitting the preacher's description and placed him in jail.

When this robbery occurred, the drivers were W. J. Ellis and Al Jacks. A diverse group of passengers included Mike Jacobs and M. Lasker of Galveston, Henry Copleton of Cincinnati, L. Pandro of Tyler, William Bailey of Fort Worth, J. H. Burney of Colorado, Charles Vroman Eugene Cartledge of San Angelo, J. G. Mueller of Uvalde, and R. W. Rose of Fort Concho.

The highwayman was quite jovial as he put sacks over the passengers' heads so they couldn't identify him as the robber, and then he demanded their money. Some passengers hid their valuables from him successfully while others didn't. The robber complimented the people on their bravery and wrote the following affidavit, "This is to certify that the passengers of the San Angelo-Ballinger stage line on April 20 were no cowards, as they would have fought if they had had a chance - Rube Burris."

The passengers had an extended time to visit with the robber because he made them stall until the stage coming from Ballinger made its appearance. During the five-hour wait, the thief made passenger Mike Jacobs distribute his cigars to the crowd. The robber enjoyed the wait as he joked with everybody.

One of the two preachers on the stage became angry when the robber demanded their valuables. This preacher said, "Sir, I believe I know you and I think you have heard me preach." One rider told the preacher if his sermons bore such fruit, he didn't think he would go hear him again. This comment didn't make the man of God very happy.

Within a few hours, United States Marshals questioned the passengers who rode the ill-fated stage. The driver W. J. Ellis mentioned that he had lost a one hundred dollar bill to the thief. A short time later, a twenty-six year old cowboy named

James Albert Newsome was found to have such a bill in his possession. James worked on ranches in Runnels County. With little evidence other than the one hundred dollar bill, the law arrested James and put him in jail.

When he was tried in Waco, Texas on December 9, 1887, the young cowboy was convicted for the robbery. James had two other indictments against him that said he robbed the stage on the same route on September 29, four hours before the one he was convicted of. Supposedly he also robbed the stage on October 5, five days later. He was sentenced to 99 years in prison even though he had twelve witnesses who swore he was attending a rodeo some 45 miles away at the time of the first alleged robbery.

Since the preacher's testimony caused an innocent man to be convicted of the crime, the real Rube Burris(Burroughs) discovered that a man was serving time for a robbery he pulled. To right the wrong committed by the preacher, Rube robbed the same stagecoach driven by W. J. Ellis April 5, 1888. When the robbery was completed and valuables were taken from 14 passengers, Rube told Ellis that the wrong man was in jail for a holdup involving the two preachers. The outlaw described the robbery in question and told how many passengers were there and what had been taken from them. To prove he was familiar with Ellis' stagecoach, Rube looked at his team of horses and asked, "Aren't you driving the same team, Tom and Jerry, that you drove when the stage was robbed before?"

Ellis admitted that he was. "But you have them hitched up wrong," said the bandit. "Tom belongs on the other side and Jerry over here." Ellis looked at the team and realized that Rube was right. He also admitted to authorities that the stage robber was short and looked nothing like the man who was in jail. Ellis made an affidavit concerning these happenings and sent it to the U. S. Supreme Court. Newsome had a new trial and was acquitted. Ellis' testimony reversed the charges on the innocent man.

When Ellis wasn't worrying over robbers, he enjoyed his passengers. The C. D. Foote family came to Ben Ficklin in 1876 and their daughter Gula was a feisty nine-year old at the time. In her diary she admits her early fear of Indians, rattlesnakes, horses, and skunks. But she quickly overcame her scare of horses when W. J. Ellis let her ride on his big stagecoach. When he had emptied his load of passengers in the Ben Ficklin community, Gula met him, and he let her ride to the corrals on the stage.

During the stagecoach days, Peg-Leg Crossing near Menardville was only a mile from Robber's Roost, a place that was famous for the number of holdups that occurred. This crossing on the San Saba was twelve miles east of Menardville. Robber's Roost was the name given the high cliffs above the river. The stagecoach road ran parallel to the high cliffs, so any travelers were hemmed in with the cliffs on one side and the San Saba River running on the other. High grass growing along the road made it even harder for stage passengers to see their surroundings.

Milam Taylor and his family kept the stage stop at Peg Leg Crossing. The Taylors penned the stage horses in their stable ready to take the next leg of the journey. They not only fed the horses, but also prepared a meal for the stage driver and any passengers who cared to eat. One observer at that time remembered the red stage passing through Peg Leg rocking and swaying on its springs. Mrs. A. W. Noguess said, "It was almost like riding a pitching horse to ride in one of them."

Mrs. Noguess remembered riding the stage as late as the summer of 1877. She said, "I came up from school at Fort Mason to Peg Leg on the old red stage drawn by four horses."

Mrs. Lovena Hanson Brown also remembered riding a stage from Fredericksburg to Peg Leg Crossing in 1879. She said, "The stagecoach was hauled by six horses and had room inside for nine passengers. Also two guards rode up above on the coach, beside the driver. The stages were often held up and robbed in those days so all the passengers were armed as were the guards. Since there were no banks in this country then, money was sent in mail sacks. Robberies were plentiful, robbing both the passengers and the mail sacks."

As early as 1878, stage agents used the telegraph to relay messages. T. P Lockhart, stage agent at Mason, received a message July 6, 1878, with the words he hated to hear: "Buckboard was stopped and mail robbed last night two miles west of Peg Leg."

Rube Burris who frequently robbed stages near San Angelo also showed up at the Peg-Leg Station outside of Menard quite regularly. Writers in newspapers who described his hold-ups called Rube the "gentleman bandit" because he seemed to have book learning and went about his profession in a business like way. He was so polite to his victims that some stage riders said it was an honor to be held up by him.

Rube was mysterious because no one ever saw him until he suddenly appeared in front of the stage. He pointed his gun at the driver and told the passengers to "get out and line up." Usually he held up the stage at night, so it was easier for him to disappear. He kept his face covered and a blanket on his horse. He had an unusual habit of putting dunce caps over the heads of his victims while he ran his fingers through their pockets.

He was as accommodating to his victims as possible. When he took money from some people, they complained that they had no more money. One passenger told Rube that after the robbery he did not have enough money for breakfast. At this remark, Rube gave the man 50 cents. The robber also told his victims that he would try to hurry so that they would not be late for their train connection.

Rube Burris continued to rob stages until he was captured and put in the penitentiary in Austin. His wife had permission to bring food to Rube every day that he was incarcerated. She met her husband in the area of the jail called the "bull pen." One day she placed a pistol in one hand and held it under the basket. As she brought the container of food in front of the Sheriff so he could examine the contents, she told him the handle was broken and that was the reason she had her hand under the basket.

Rube escaped, and his wife was arrested. The grand jury never indicted her because they explained that a wife ought to help her husband. They blamed the Sheriff for negligence.

Some people who read the San Angelo paper and kept up with Rube, began to wonder in the summer of 1888 if he was gone from the area for good. Although stagecoaches still carried people from town to town, the railroad workers were making big strides in bringing a railroad to San Angelo. One observer remarked, "If Rube Burrows don't hurry up, the railroad will be finished before he can make another play on the stage."

A lone bandit said, "Well, boys, I am here," as a stage stopped again on this notorious road. Around midnight on October 1, 1887, the masked man hit the stage between Ballinger and San Angelo as it neared Nicholas' pasture. This holdup was close to the Willow Water Hole. Even though he was covered by the dark of night, the robber had each passenger stand in a line as he placed a cap over their head. The outlaw demanded they stand with hands high as he emptied their pockets, one by one.

Mrs. M. E. Collard of San Angelo rode that stage and identified the bandit as the same one that had held up a stage she was riding the previous week. One man who had been insulted by the robbery was J. C. Raas. He was heard to say that if he ever rode that stage between Ballinger and San Angelo again, he would carry his shotgun with him and "dispute the matter with the road agent."

News of these robberies in Tom Green County spread more than two hundred miles away where they were read in the *Dallas Morning News*. In one such robbery between San Angelo and Ballinger, the Dallas writer described the robber as, "one man, about 5 feet 8 inches in height, light complexion, weight about 135 pounds, wore dark soft hat, apparently wore light-colored jeans pushed into boots, light-colored coat, large red handkerchief over the face." The outlaw's horse was not to be left out as he was described as a dark brown pony that was about 14 hands high carrying a half-rigged saddle that was well worn but nickel-plated.

The money taken by the robber was identified as follows:
United States notes, series 1880, of the following numbers: A 1,102, 260, check letter 203 pd. $20; A 525, 840, check letter 11C, $20; A 417,672 C, check letter 8 D, $20; Z, 18, 140,399, check letter C, $5.

J. W. Johnson who was the Sheriff of Tom Green County posted a $200 reward if this robber was captured and convicted. He was elusive though and remained free to rob again.

Other areas of Texas had their share of stage robbers. The Austin to San Antonio stage line had plenty holdups and unpleasant events also. The line could boast that in 1874, it was held up by some of the most famous outlaws of all – the Jesse James gang. For Jesse to be near Austin was a rarity because he usually kept a low profile in Texas. A year or so before the holdup, Jesse James rode through West Texas on a trip to visit Drury Woodson James in California. He was impressed with the grass available west of the Concho River area. For a brief time, it was confirmed that

Jesse and Frank James ran horses on a ranch near Sterling City. This ranch was about forty-five miles northwest of Fort Concho.

On April 7, 1874, the soon-to-be targeted stage left San Antonio with some distinguished riders. Travelers included Right Reverend Bishop Gregg of the Episcopal Diocese of Texas and George Breckenridge, president of the First National Bank of San Antonio. Crammed into this stage were also six other men and three ladies. The beautiful day started well as the team of four horses pulled out on the road leaving San Antonio as they headed toward Austin. Such a diverse group of passengers kept

Robber ready to attack during a reenactment at the Jesse James-Younger Conference near Sterling City on October 5, 2001. Author's Collection.

the conversation lively and political sides of each question brought much debate. As the day progressed, most of the political, as well as religious issues of the day had been thoroughly hashed. With a stop or two to stretch their legs, the men and women felt the time in the stagecoach had been rather pleasant. Best of all was the fact that they didn't hit any deep mud holes or have to swim any swollen streams.

But when they had traveled all day, the shadows of dusk approached while they were still 25 miles from Austin. At that time, the stage driver noticed a group of men wearing sombreros and approaching him on horseback. This was a common sight in that area of Texas, so he thought little about it until two of them rode along side the stagecoach saying, "Halt."

The bandits ordered passengers to step out of the stage as they pulled trunks open and scattered the mail about the ground. After pilfering through the mail and the luggage, the robbers turned their attention to the passengers and demanded their valuables. The Bishop pleaded with the robbers to not take his money and his watch. One robber replied, "Christ didn't have any watch, and he didn't ride in a stagecoach. He walked about doing his Father's will." That particular robber knew some Bible as he explained that he was not a Christian, but rather a Philistine.

This outlaw life that the James brothers lived was a far cry from the way they were raised as God-fearing children. Jesse James' father, Robert James, attended Georgetown College in Georgetown, Kentucky where he studied to develop his preaching skills. Young men like Robert preached as soon as they received the call from God. Obviously the James family heard him preach and recite scripture at home. Robert James started a school called William Jewell College, but his death at the hands of Union soldiers changed the James clan's direction. Young Jesse saw his father hanged by the soldiers who invaded their little Kentucky farm and never could overcome the hatred he felt. After fighting for the Confederacy, Jesse took on the life of an outlaw.

The robbers were successful in their Austin holdup. The banker Brackenridge lost $1,000, a gold watch, and a diamond pin. Although the robbers were harsh with some passengers, they showed compassion when one lady said they were taking all the money she had. The bandits apologized and gave her money back to her. The robbers swore at the passengers as well as joked with them for about two hours while they took over $3,000 of cash from them.

Some time later, robber Jim Reed was mortally wounded in another incident. Before he died, Jim admitted that he helped rob the stage near Austin on April 7, 1874, with the help of "men from Missouri." Such a description could mean only one gang, so most people believed that he referred to Frank and Jesse James along with Cole, Bob, and Jim Younger.

The stage line from Austin to Burnet ran by a stage stop called Rutledge, which was northwest of Austin. This location, where passengers stopped and stretched their legs, was in southwestern Williamson County. Eventually the railroads made their way to this area in 1882 and the Rutledge village moved one mile east of the stage station.

When the move took place, business didn't look too good for stage owners. The community of Rutledge was finally wiped away, and all that is left of that stage stop location is the intersection of U. S. Highway 183 and Ranch Road 620.

The same Episcopal minister, Bishop Gregg, who had been held up by the James gang, took another trip on a stage by himself from San Antonio to San Marcos. A robber stopped the stage and demanded the Bishop's watch. Seems like he had a hard time keeping watches. The Bishop pleaded with the outlaw and said, "My watch is old and would be of little or no value to you but it is of great value to me on account of the many pleasant memories associated with it."

The Bishop talked some more to the robber and said, "I therefore, beg you not to force me to give it up. Also I have very little money, barely enough to carry me through this trip. You see a preacher is always a poor man."

The robber became curious and asked him to which church did he belong. The Bishop replied, "I am a Bishop of the Episcopal Church." When he heard that reply, the bandit explained that he was also an Episcopalian. Even some crooks must have a conscious because the masked man apologized to the Bishop for bothering him.

During these dangerous years of the 1800s, robbers definitely kept stage rides from being too monotonous. More than a few of the holdup men were incarcerated, but some lived to be old men, such as Rube Burris.

Robbers made their living the way they could while stage station managers made theirs. Both groups saw a lot of the Texas countryside when it was sparsely populated. Each station was separated from the next by the distance a team could travel while pulling the stage.

Jesse James at the age of 17 when he was fighting for the Confederacy.

Chapter 10: Stage Stations

A Texas Ranger named Captain J. B. Gillett described how the stage stations appeared that he saw along the route from San Antonio to El Paso. He said most of the buildings were adobe with two separate rooms connected with a passageway. Gillett explained that one room was used for cooking and serving the meals, whereas the other large room was for sleeping. The corral holding horses or mules lay behind the adobe station. Its walls of two feet thick adobe reached eight feet high to provide protection. The man overseeing this station was called a tender. He charged 50 cents for a meal and retained the income from this accommodation to the riders.

Some stage stations, near active forts, were very small in size. They had room only for the mail and cargo that was to be carried on the next stage. Their replacement horses may have shared the corral with the cavalry's mounts.

The stage stop ruins at Fort Chadbourne suggests that the building was made of stone, but wasn't large in size. Photo by the author.

Occasionally the same room that held the mail also made-do as a kitchen for the travelers. Fort Chadbourne had a stone building for its stage stop, but the size of the ruins suggests that the travelers had to eat in close quarters.

When the Indians caused a lot of ruckus along the stage lines, military personnel were called in to guard the stages. In West Texas there were several companies of Black soldiers who also helped the stagecoaches make their daily routes successfully. The Indians called these troopers buffalo soldiers because their hair was curly and because they fought so valiantly. Occasionally a trooper was left at the end of the line without a way home; that is, he had no horse.

Therefore, riding the stage was the logical way back to his fort. However, segregation made life very hard for the black troopers. Col. Shafter sent instructions down the stage lines that Blacks "could use the facilities at the way stations and ride the coaches back to their posts."

Rancher W. Black rode the same stage line that passed through Christoval, as well as Menard and Fort McKavett. In 1875, Col. William Black bought a ranch near Fort McKavett. All his trips to Texas from his home in St. Louis were made by stage. One of the stops nearby was on the Menard-McKavett road at the old Ben Ellis ranch. Although Col. Black never was robbed by outlaws, his son-in-law, R. S. Kinslow, was.

Buffalo Soldiers such as these men rode guard to protect the stagecoaches from Indians in West Texas. Photo taken in the 1890s is courtesy of *San Angelo Standard Times.*

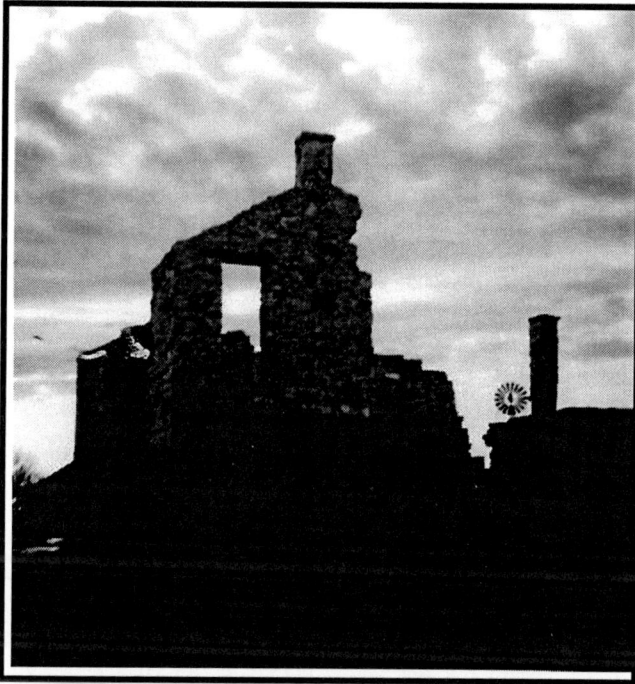

Picture of the two-storied Oficers Quarters' ruins at Fort McKavett. This fort, like many others in Texas, was a stage station. Photo made by Sharon Gentry.

The stage was near the community named Celery when the robbers appeared. The driver decided to keep going when the robbers told him to stop. The bandits let loose with a volley of shots that barely missed Winslow's head. Peg-Leg Station, situated 12 miles east of Menard, was a fordable crossing on the San Saba River where McDougal Creek runs into it. Long before stagecoaches made their way there to change horses, Spanish travelers made their way across the river here in the 1700s. It was a common campground for Indians, German settlers, and mustang hunters. This ford was used by the Immigration Road to California during the gold rush and finally used as a stage station for the San Antonio-El Paso Mail from 1867 to 1888. The station itself was situated on a hill overlooking the ford.

Thomas Will Ward was probably the man named Peg-Leg. He was a hero in the battle at San Jacinto, and years later he attended an anniversary celebration of the famous battle. When a cannon fired, Ward's leg was blown off. Ward was fitted with an artificial leg so he could walk. His wooden stump was long and straight so he had to swing it around to navigate very well. Although he lived at the stage stop bearing his name, in later years he became Land Commissioner of Texas.

This stage stop was located in an open pasture about one or two miles wide and four miles long that lay along the San Saba River. This area was called Peg-leg Pocket. It was sparsely populated, and only one or two families lived at the stage stop. For that reason, robberies happened here more than once. In 1877 a young lieutenant named Harry Kirby rode the stage one hundred eighty miles from San Antonio to Fort McKavett where he was stationed. He spent the night in Fredericksburg and at five in the morning was ushered into a scaled-down version of coach that had only cloth curtains on each side.

Riding with him was a Judge Blacker and a Jew from New Orleans. As he had ridden the stage all day, Kirby began to doze about 11 p.m. Suddenly a man yelled at the driver to stop. The young Lieutenant grabbed a pistol he had and planned to defend himself. The knowledgeable Judge persuaded him to put the gun up because there were too many robbers. Hurriedly the passengers tried to hide their money in their shoes or in the coach. One by one the robbers ordered the men out of the stage and searched them. When little money was found, the robbers searched the coach.

Finally the passengers were ordered to pull off their boots. Lieutenant Kirby carefully placed his foot on a roll of money and saved some of his cash due to the darkness of the night. He was relieved to be ordered back in the stage and ride onward to the Fort without any other mishap.

Robbers weren't the only problem that passengers encountered. Many times the stage was over crowded, and the road was very rough. Often times the driver made stage riders get out and walk, supposedly to rest the horses.

While mentioning the rough roads, the question arises as to who built the stage roads during the 1800s? Builders most likely came from the nearby forts. Some men stationed at various military forts around Texas complained as loud as they dared about being used to build roads instead of fighting Indians. To move big boulders out of the road, men had a pick and a shovel. If a stage passed over a rocky road, the metal around the wheels dug a rut in the rock several inches deep. Such roads added to the traveler's misery, so the workers made the roads as smooth as possible.

C. Bain used the newspapers such as the *Concho Times* to advertise his stagecoach routes from San Angelo to San Antonio and Austin as this article indicates:

"From Fort Concho (i.e. San Angelo) four-horse coaches and two horse hacks on alternate days, via Ben Ficklin, Fort McKavett, Menardville, Mason, Fredericksburg and Boerne. Thence four-horse coaches seven times a week to San Antonio. Daily coach from Fredericksburg, via Blanco, to Austin. From Fort Concho (San Angelo) four-horse coaches and hacks, via Fort Stockton, Fort Davis, Fort Quitman, San Elizario, Socorro, Ysleta, to El Paso, connecting with stages to Chihuahua, Mexico, and to Mesilla, connecting with stages to Silver City, Tucson and Fort Yuma, Arizona; Las Cruces, Albuquerque and Santa Fe, New Mexico.

Carrying packages to all points (except money). Careful and polite drivers, first-class coaches and stock, fully guaranteeing comfort and satisfaction to passengers. For information and tickets apply to / F. B. Gray. / at W. S. Veck's store."

Stages passing through Menard and Peg-leg often continued to Llano. On October 6, 1884, the driver had his horses moving toward Llano when a bandit by the side of the rode fired his Winchester twice. This noise got the driver's attention as he pulled on the reins to stop the stage. The highwayman discussed what articles he expected from the passengers, including their money. After passengers obeyed the robber and gave him their money, he was a hundred dollars richer. He also rummaged through the mail bags to retreat anything valuable before he released the stage to continue its journey.

As the stages passed her house all during the day and night, Mrs. Noguess realized how heavy the traffic was on the San Antonio-El Paso road. Mrs. Noguess noticed the large number of people riding the stage. She said that sometimes the stage was so full that the driver boosted one or two big boys on top to ride with him.

Will M. Johnson of Menard opened the Rock Saloon there in 1888. Since the town had no bank, occasionally he had to take large bills and checks to San Antonio so he could exchange them for smaller bills and silver. He also handled exchanges for his neighbors while on the trip. On one such dash back from San Antonio, Johnson rode the stage successfully to a location near Llano on his way home. While he was rather drunk from imbibing some whiskey along the way, the stage was held up by a masked robber. Acting in Mr. Johnson's favor was the fact that before the drinking took effect on Mr. Johnson, he had hidden his sack of money in the bottom of the coach and covered it with straw.

The robber told everybody to be quiet while he took their valuables. Johnson thought he recognized the thief, so he was not surprised when the robber started to remove his watch and stopped when he saw Will Johnson's initials. Mr. Johnson did not obey the robber's request for passengers to be quiet when he said, "I've just been to San Antonio and spent all my money so I haven't any. I was on my way home now." When he told the story later to his family, they figured that he was so drunk that he had forgotten the money. The robber tore opened the U. S. mailbags and found a bit more money before he disappeared, but he never found Mr. Johnson's cash.

This picture of the Splittgerber Stage Station west of Menard was taken in the late eighties by Noah Rose. Photo is Courtesy of Mayon Neal whose mother-in-law, Winnie Bible Ellis Neal, owned the property where the stand was located.

The Splittgerber Station was probably built in the latter part of 1868 or 1869 because it was used by freighters also. Adams and Wicks of San Antonio received a freighting contract to haul supplies to Fort Concho. This stage stop was used on the San Antonio to San Angelo Route, which passed through Peg-Leg Station, Menard, Splittgerber, and then Fort McKavett. Splittgerber was six or seven miles west of Menard and was conveniently situated near a spring.

Although this stage stop carried the name "Splittgerber" after landowner Oscar Splittgerber, another person ran the station at one time. His name was Tom Embry, and he had a midget daughter as well as a son named Jap Embry.

Eventually, Oscar Splittgerber's wife Martha helped him run the ranch and the stage stop. At one time, their ranch house was on the south side of the road perched on a knoll, and the stage stop was on the north. Later they moved the house to the same side as the stage stop. Like so many other legends, the Splittgerber home was the center of a story stating that they had buried gold under the house during an Indian raid. For years, people dug in every direction but failed to find the treasure. Construction of Highway 29 leveled the last remains of the stage stop.

Occasionally stagecoach riders were fortunate to ride a stage owned by a man who wanted to improve the ride for his passengers. Col. T. M Thomason from Louisiana, an old stage driver himself, bought the line between Burnet and Mason. He promised several changes including more horsepower. Coaches traveling between these two towns would have four horses hooked to them. The newspaper report said, "Patrons will be more comfortable. Only the stretch between Concho and San Angelo would keep two horses for their drive."

Even though Col. Thomason wanted to make the stages more comfortable, he had little control over the robbers present in that part of Texas. Stagecoach lines criss-crossed Central Texas just as they did other parts of the state, many times leaving themselves vulnerable. Frequent robberies of stages in Lampasas and Burnet counties had lawmen on edge, but they finally captured James Pitts and Charles Yeager and declared them responsible for the holdups. Although the two men were in jail in Austin, Marshall Gosling decided to move them to San Antonio for safekeeping.

The Marshall, accompanied by deputies J. F. Maning and L. J. Loving, transported the two outlaws by way of train. Each prisoner was handcuffed to his seat, so the lawmen felt the prisoners were well confined. Two other passengers on the train sat in front of the prisoners. They were Mrs. E. A. Brown, grandmother of James Pitts, and Miss Rosa Yeager, sister of Charles Yeager. The two women were very talkative to the prisoners. After riding the train awhile, the two women left the car where the lawmen were and returned in a few minutes.

Not long after the women sat down, pistol shots sounded through out the train car. One deputy received a bullet in the neck and died. Amidst the barrage of gunfire erupting in the train car, the prisoners were able to escape. Both Mrs. Brown and James Pitts died, and only prisoner Charles Yeager was caught and taken in custody again.

One day a preacher traveling the central Texas area by way of stage decided to hide $250 in his clothing. He knew robbers often appeared on that particular road, so he wasn't surprised when the stage made an unannounced stop. The preacher had a gold watch, which the robbers spied at once. He pleaded with the bandits to let him keep his watch. They finally agreed to leave him alone since the watch was all he had. The parson convinced the robbers so well that he was penniless that he kept his money and his watch from them.

Sometimes the stage helpers piled the mail and baggage too high on top of the stage as they did one day in November of 1884. Not far down the road, the driver realized that his coach was overturning. He held the reins in his hands on his downward spin. The stage flipped on its side. Six passengers could not get out of the coach the way it landed, so they cut themselves an escape hatch. They climbed out to discover no one was seriously hurt.

Routinely, visitors from New England and Canada came to Texas to check on their misguided kin who had strayed away from the grandeur of civilized life and landed in Texas. Jose Tweedy left New York in 1876 and sailed to Galveston. He had plans to become a sheep rancher in Texas. Although he bought his sheep near Fort Clark, his ranch home was in Knickerbocker, about twenty miles southwest of Fort Concho. In November of 1884, two Canadians, J. W. Morse and William McNabb, arrived by stage to visit Mr. Tweedy at his Dove Creek Ranch.

In the Menard area, some old timers said that the best entertainment around was watching the arrival of the stage from San Antonio. The bouncing coach usually came to Menard about daylight. The four to six horses were so full of vim and vigor that they hardly stopped in Menardville, as it was called early on. The driver had to circle in front of the store several times until he successfully threw off the mail sack and grabbed the outgoing mail. This town was not a place where they changed horses. Stage stations named Peg-Leg and Splittgerber were a few miles out of Menard, and the fresh horses were exchanged at these places.

The stage driver blew his bugle when he was about a mile out of town. Sometimes he blew it so people could run outside and watch the coach come by. At other towns, he blew it to let stable hands know it was time to bring the fresh team out to the road.

Riders of these stages were more-than-ready to get out at stage stops for a rest. When the stage was a mile or two from town, the driver blew a bugle to announce their arrival. Picture drawn by Sharon Gentry.

Sometimes accidents happened to people riding the stage even though robbers were nowhere near. Frank McQueen drove the stage between San Antonio and Boerne, so on December 18, 1884, it was natural for him to stop the coach at Leon Springs. While waiting for the mailbags, he got off his box to adjust a harness. Before doing this, he tied the reins to the brake.

As Frank jumped down, he scared the horses, and they took off down the road running. Frank hung to the right wheel horse for several yards and tried to turn them. Since he was unable to control the horses, Frank was thrown off and landed on some rocks. This accident broke his neck, and he died quickly. A passenger named Mr. McDonald from New York was in the run-away stage also. He decided the right thing to do was to jump out the window. He survived with a broken leg. Mr. and Mrs.

The stage station at the Pinery is only rock ruins. This stop had several well-made buildings that acted as a fort when the Butterfield Mail Route passed by in 1868. Photo made by Bob Tate.

Russell were still in the fast moving stage with their two children when everyone else had departed. Russell shot the wheel horse, which slowed the coach enough that he threw the two children out the window to safety.

The dead horse caused the other animals to run in a circling pattern until they overturned the stage. This accident finally released the harness and freed the horses. Mr. and Mrs. Russell survived the severe shaking they endured, and their children only had minor bruises. No matter where stages went, the trip could be very scary and sometimes fatal. The sadness of the driver, Frank McQueen's, death touched the lives of all the passengers as well as stage hands. Even so, the travelers had to change vehicles and continue their trip.

One of the most desolate areas to drive through was the stagecoach trip from Fort Stockton to El Paso. This journey was part of the famous San Antonio to El Paso Stage Line. As the stages pointed their horses westward on this trail, they crossed the Chichuachua Trail, which moved north from the Rio Grande. Anything could happen in these remote areas, so many trips were made with escorts. Whether the stage routes passed through communities that were large or small, all the towns depended on the mail service and passenger transportation. Although early-day settlers eagerly anticipated each arrival of the stagecoaches when they were rolling across the hills and valleys of Texas, they are now gone forever. Stagecoaches are etched only in our memories as an important mode of travel.

Bibliography

Books

Carter, Capt. R. G. *On the Border with Mackenzie,* Eynon Printing Co.: Washington D. C., 1935.

Claton, Mary. "Trailing the Stages Through Crockett County," *A History of Crockett County.*

Conkling, Roscoe P. and Margaret B. *The Butterfield Overland Mail, 1857 – 1869.* Glendale, California: Clark, 1947.

Crawford, Leta. *A History of Irion County.* Waco: Texian Press, 1966.

Locklin, Nora. *63 Years of Married Life on the West Texas Plains,* McCamey, Texas, 1987.

Dearen, Patrick, *Crossing the Pecos,* Fort Worth: Texas Christian Univ. Press, 1996.

Flatt, Travis D. *The History of the Dearton Family.*

Gillett, Captain J. B., *Six Years with the Texas Rangers,* Kerrville: 1934.

Loomis, John, *Texas Ranchman, The Memoirs of John Loomis,* Chadron: the Fur Press, 1982.

Moody, Ralph. *Stagecoach West.* Lincoln: University of Nebraska Press, 1998.

Oatman, Wilburn, "Bluffton," *Llano Gem of the Hill Country.* Hereford: PioneerBook Publishers, Inc., 1970.

Oehler, Herbert E., *Hill Country Boy,* Kerrville: Herring Printing Company, 1974.

Pecos County Historical Commission, "Camp Melvin," *Pecos County History,* Staked Plains Press, 1984.

Pierce, V. I. *Yesteryear.* San Angelo: Talley Press, 1980.

Poe, Charlsie, *Runnels is My County,* San Antonio: The Naylor Co., 1970.

Rister, Carl C. *Fort Griffin on the Texas Frontier,* Norman: University of Oklahoma, 1956.

Santleban, August, *A Texas Pioneer,* New York: The Neale Publishing Co., 1910.

Schleicher County History Society, *A History of Schleicher County, Texas.* San Angelo: Anchor Publishing Company, 1979.

St. Clair, Kathleen E. and Clifton, eds. *Little Towns of Texas,* Jacksonville, Texas:

Jayroe Graphics Arts, 1982.

Tom Green County Historical Preservation League. "The Origins and History of Tom Green County," *Tom Green County Chronicles of Our Heritage, Vol. 1* . Abilene: H. V. Chapman & Sons, 2003.

Warner, Ezra J. *Generals in Gray*, Baton Rouge: Louisiana State University Press, 1959.

Williams, Clayton, *Texas' Last Frontier: Fort Stockton and the Trans-Pecos, 1861 – 1895.* College Station: Texas A & M University Press, 1982.

Wooster, Robert, *Soldiers, Sutlers, and Settlers.* College Station: Texas A & M Univ. Press.

1912 Worley's San Angelo City Directory, Vol. 5

Interviews & Speeches

A visit with Jim Ridge, son-in-law to M.D. Bryant at the M.D. Bryant Trust's pasture August 29, 2004.

An interview with Bob Hedrick, September 22, 2004, at Knickerbocker, Texas.

An interview with Jay Farris, October 19, 2004, Knickerbocker, TX.

An interview with Dorothy Robertson at the Comanche Museum, August 29, 2004.

An interview with Suzanne Campbell, at ASU May 3, 2005, San Angelo, Texas.

Talk with Drew Sykes on August 5, 2006 concerning the Tweedy Pasture marker.

Telephone Interview with Burl Pringle, January 12, 2005.

Talk given by Jim Davis in Sterling City Texas, October 5, 2001.

Talked with De Witt Ayers in San Angelo, Texas, April 10, 2005.

Talked with Troy Williams near Alpine, Texas, July 27, 2004.

Speech given by Glenn Ely, "Stagecoaching in Tom Green County" at the West Texas Historical Meeting, April 5, 2002.

Magazines

Ellis, W. J. "Tells of Depredations of Early Day Robber *Frontier Times,* October 14, 1978.

Fauntleroy, J. D. "Old Stage Routes of Texas," *Frontier Times,* July, 1929, Vol. 6.

Hunter, Marvin, "Jesse James," *Frontier Times,* July,1945, Vol. 22.

Hunter, Marvin, "The Old Butterfield Stage Line,"*Frontier Times,* June, 1945, Vol. 22.

Poe,Charlsie, "Bob Holland, Old-Time Cowboy," *True West,* Fall, 1981.

Sanderson, Donna Henry, "Heritage of the Blackwell Area," *Ranch & Rural Living Magazine,* April, 2006.

"The Old Horsehead Crossing on the Pecos," *Ranch and Rural Living Magazine,* November, 1952.

Williams, J. W. "The Butterfield Overland Mail Road Across Texas," *Southwestern Historical Quarterly,* Vol. LXI, July 1957.

Newspapers

Ballinger & Menardville Stage Line, *The Concho Herald,* October 2, 1890.

"Sheriff's Department," October 1, 1887 and "Well Boys, I am Here," October 5, 1887, *Dallas Morning News.*

Frontier Echo, February 23, 1877.

"Newton, Watson, Savell Surviving Stage Drivers." *San Angelo Standard Times,* 70 Anniversary Edition.

"Stagecoaches Operated by Three Men." *San Angelo Standard Times,* July 4, 1976.

Childress, Carrie, "A History of Sipe Springs," *Comanche Chief's Golden Anniversary Edition,* May 29, 1924.

Unpublished Manuscripts and Files

Christopher, Iona Lea, "History of Irion County," theme written during the 1935-36 Mertzon H.S. year.

Fundersmith, Connie, "Knickerbocker In Its Heyday From 1890 – 1913."

McMillan, Clarice Atkins "History of Christoval, Texas, 1874 – 1968.

"Old Stage Stand Near Ben Ficklin," Susan Miles Scrapbook Collection, West Texas Collection at Angelo state University.

"Stagecoach Files," Heart of Texas Museum, Colorado City, Texas.

"Stagecoach Files," Fort Concho Museum, San Angelo, Texas.

INDEX

CPSIA information can be obtained at www.ICGtesting.com
Printed in the USA
BVOW04s1904210114

342590BV00003B/203/P